TAMIL NADU

A STATE STUDY GUIDE

REVATHI SUBRAMANYAM

Published by

Hawk Press
4836/24, Ansari Road, Daryaganj
New Delhi – 110 002
Phones: 91-11-23278618, 91-11-43667199
E-mail: thehawkpress@gmail.com
www.thehawkpress.com

ISBN: 978-93-88318-86-0

Preface

Tamil Nadu, state of India, located in the extreme south of the subcontinent. It is bounded by the Indian Ocean to the east and south and by the states of Kerala to the west, Karnataka (formerly Mysore) to the northwest, and Andhra Pradesh to the north. Enclosed by Tamil Nadu along the north-central coast are the enclaves of Puducherry and Karaikal, both of which are part of Puducherry union territory. The capital is Chennai (Madras), on the coast in the northeastern portion of the state.

The present publication shows how the individuals, Palayams, made tremendous sacrifice to achieve their goals. The series of events which followed in the Southern District of Ramnad, Madurai and Thirunulveli may be collectively called the Palaiyagar rebellion, since the events are mostly their rising against the collecting authority of the English. The perpetual warfare all over the region left no room for any profitable social activity.

The State of Tamil Nadu has a hoary antiquity. Though early sangam classics throw historical references, we pass to recorded history only from the Pallavas. The southern states of India were under the hegemony of the Cholas, the Cheras and the Pandyas for centuries. The Pallavas held supremacy from about the second quarter of the fourth century A.D. They were the originators of the famous Dravidian style of temple architecture. The last Pallava ruler was Aparajita, in whose reign the later Cholas under Vijayalaya and Aditya asserted themselves by about the 10th century. At the end of the 11th century, Tamil Nadu was ruled by several dynasties like the Chalukyas, Cholas and Pandyas. In the two centuries that followed, the imperial Cholas gained paramountcy over South India.

ABOUT THE BOOK

The State of Tamil Nadu has a hoary antiquity. Though early sangam classics throw historical references, we pass to recorded history only from the Pallavas. The southern states of India were under the hegemony of the Cholas, the Cheras and the Pandyas for centuries. The Pallavas held supremacy from about the second quarter of the fourth century A.D. They were the originators of the famous Dravidian style of temple architecture. The last Pallava ruler was Aparajita, in whose reign the later Cholas under Vijayalaya and Aditya asserted themselves by about the 10th century. At the end of the 11th century, Tamil Nadu was ruled by several dynasties like the Chalukyas, Cholas and Pandyas. In the two centuries that followed, the imperial Cholas gained paramountcy over South India. Muslims gradually strengthened their position, which led to the establishment of the Bahamani Sultanate, by the middle of the 14th century. At the same time, the Vijayanagar Kingdom quickly consolidated itself and extended its sway over the whole of South India, and at the close of the century, Vijayanagar became the supreme power in South. However, it crumbled at the battle of Talikota in 1564 to the confederate forces of the Deccan Sultans. The structure of the government of Tamil Nadu, like that of most other states of India, is determined by the national constitution of 1950. The head of state is the governor, who is appointed by the president of India. The book is of great utility to students, teachers, tourists, guides and general readers.

Contents

1

State at a Glance

Tamil is a state at the southern tip of India. Tamil Nadu is bordered by Puducherry, Kerala, Karnataka and Andhra Pradesh. Tamil Nadu has had continuous human habitation since pre-historic times. Its long history and cultural traditions are among the oldest in the world. The ancient Tamil kingdoms of Chera, Chola, Pallava and Pandya are of very ancient origins. They patronised a mature culture which produced some of the oldest surviving literature in India.

Colonised by the East India Company, Tamil Nadu was eventually incorporated into the Madras Presidency. After the independence of India, the Madras State was created in 1956 based on linguistic boundaries. The name of the Madras State was changed to Tamil Nadu in the year 1969. The politics of Tamil Nadu has been dominated by DMK and AIADMK, who are of the Dravidian movement which agitated demanding concessions for the 'Dravidian' population of Tamil Nadu.

Lying on a low plain along the southeastern coast of the Indian peninsula, Tamil Nadu is bounded by the Eastern Ghats in the north and Nilgiri, Annamalai Hills, and Palakkad on the west. The state has large fertile areas along the Coromandel coast, the Palk strait, and the Gulf of Mannar. The fertile plains of Tamil Nadu are fed by rivers such as Kaveri, Palar, and Vaigai, and by the northeast monsoon. Traditionally a manufacturing state, Tamil Nadu is also a leading producer of agricultural products.

The sixth most populous state in the Indian Union, Tamil Nadu has the largest urban agglomeration nationwide. Increases in literacy have caused Tamil Nadu to report the second lowest growth in population in India for the last decade. Globalisation brought increased export opportunities, making Tamil Nadu the fifth largest economy among the states of India. In spite of all these TN has the most number of HIV positives in India declared in 2007. The growing demands for skilled labour have caused the increased number of educational institutions in Tamil Nadu. It has the highest number of vocational training institutions in India. Chennai, which was known until 1996 as Madras, is the fourth largest city of India and the state capital. Coimbatore, Madurai, Tiruchirapalli, Salem and Tirunelveli are other large cities (Corporations) of Tamil Nadu.

The art and culture of Tamils are among the oldest in the world. Great literature, music, dance and architecture have evolved from Tamil Nadu over the past two millennia. Tamil Nadu provided the cradle in which the rich musical tradition of Carnatic music evolved. Many of the great composers such as Tyagaraja lived and flourished in Tamil Nadu.

Tamil Nadu's history dates back pre-historic times and archaeological evidence points to this area being one of the longest continuous habitations in India. From early pre-history Tamil Nadu was the home of the four powerful Tamil kingdoms of the Chera, Chola, Pandya and Pallavas. The oldest extant literature, dated between 500 BC and 200 CE mentions the exploits of the kings and the princes, and of the poets who extolled them. The early Cholas reigned between 1st and 4th centuries CE. An unknown dynasty called Kalabhras invaded and displaced the three Tamil kingdoms between the fourth and the seventh centuries CE. This is referred to as the dark age in Tamil history. They were eventually expelled by the Pandyas and the Pallavas. Around 580 CE, the Pallavas, great temple builders, emerged into prominence and dominated the south for another 150 years. They ruled a large portion of Tamil Nadu with Kanchipuram as their base. They subjugated the Cholas and reigned as far as the Kaveri River. Among the greatest Pallava rulers were Mahendravarman I and his son Narasimhavarman I. Dravidian architecture reached its epitome during Pallava rule.

The Cholas again rose to power by the 9th century. Under Rajaraja Chola and his son Rajendra Chola, the Cholas rose as a notable power in Asia. The Chola Empire stretched as far as Bengal. Rajaraja Chola conquered peninsular South India, and annexed parts of Sri Lanka. Rajendra Chola's navies went beyond, occupying coastal Burma, the Andaman and Nicobar Islands, Lakshadweep, Sumatra, Java, Malaya in South East Asia and Pegu islands. He defeated Mahipala, the king of the Bengal, and to commemorate his victory he built a new capital named it Gangaikonda Cholapuram.

The Cholas revelled in building magnificent temples. Brihadisvara Temple in Thanjavur is a classical example of the magnificent architecture of the Chola kingdom. Another example is the Chidambaram Temple in the heart of the temple town of Chidambaram. The power of the Cholas declined around the 13th century. With the decline of the Cholas, the Pandyas rose to prominence once again in the early 14th century.

This was short lived; they were soon subdued by Muslim Khilji invaders from the north in 1316. Madurai was sacked. The invasion led to the establishment of the Madurai Sultanate. These Muslim invasions caused the establishment of Vijayanagara Empire in the Deccan. It eventually conquered the entire Tamil country (c. 1370 CE). As the Vijayanagara Empire went into decline after mid-16th century, the Nayak governors, who were appointed by the Vijayanagar kingdom to administer various territories of the empire, declared their independence. The Nayaks of Madurai and Nayaks of Thanjavur were most prominent of them all. They reconstructed some of the oldest temples in the country.

Around 1609, the Dutch established a settlement in Pulicat. In 1639, the British, under the British East India Company, established a settlement further south, in present day Chennai. The British used petty quarrels among the provincial rulers (divide and rule) to expand their sphere of influence.

The British fought and reduced the French dominions in India to Pondicherry. They consolidated southern India into the Madras Presidency. Some notable chieftains or Poligars who fought the British East India Company as it was expanding were Veerapandya Kattabomman, Maruthu Pandiyar, Pulithevan and Dheeran Chinnamalai. Pudukkottai remained as a princely state under British suzerainty.

When India became independent in 1947, Madras Presidency became Madras State, comprising of present day Tamil Nadu, coastal Andhra Pradesh, northern Karnataka, and parts of Kerala. The state was subsequently split up along linguistic lines. In 1968, Madras State was renamed Tamil Nadu, meaning Land of Tamil.

The region of Tamil Nadu has been under continuous human habitation since prehistoric times and the history of Tamil Nadu and the civilisation of the Tamil people are among the oldest in the world. Throughout its history, spanning from the early Palaeolithic age to the modern time, this region has coexisted with various external cultures. Except for relatively short periods in its history, the Tamil region has remained independent of external occupation.

The three Tamil dynasties of Chera, Chola and Pandya were of ancient origins. Together they ruled over this land with a unique culture and language, contributing to the growth of some of the oldest extant literature in the world. They had extensive maritime trade contacts with the Roman empire.

These three dynasties were in constant struggle with each other vying for hegemony over the land. Invasion by the Kalabhras during the third century disturbed the traditional order of the land by displacing the three ruling dynasties. These occupiers were overthrown by the resurgence of the Pandyas and the Pallavas, who restored the traditional kingdoms. The Cholas, who re-emerged from obscurity in the ninth century by defeating the Pallavas and the Pandyas, rose to become a great power and extended their empire over the entire southern peninsula. At its height the Chola empire had spread from Bengal in the northeast to Sri Lanka in the south. The Chola navy held sway over the Sri Vijaya kingdom in Southeast Asia.

Rapid changes in the political situation of the rest of India due to incursions of Muslim armies from the northwest marked a turning point in the history of Tamil Nadu. With the decline of the three ancient dynasties during the fourteenth century, the Tamil country became part of the Vijayanagara Empire. Under this empire the Telugu speaking Nayak governors ruled the Tamil land. The brief appearance of the Marathas gave way to the European trading companies, who began to appear during the seventeenth century and eventually assumed greater sway over the indigenous rulers of the land.

The Madras Presidency comprising of most of southern India was created in the eighteenth century and was ruled directly by the British East India Company. After the independence of India, the Tamil Nadu state was created based on linguistic boundaries.

HISTORY OF TAMIL NADU

The region of Tamil Nadu or Tamilakam, in the southeast of modern India, shows evidence of having had continuous human habitation from 15,000 BCE to 10,000 BCE. Throughout its history, spanning the early Upper Paleolithic age to modern times, this region has coexisted with various external cultures.

The three ancient Tamil dynasties namely Chera, Chola, and Pandya were of ancient origins. Together they ruled over this land with a unique culture and language, contributing to the growth of some of the oldest extant literature in the world. They had extensive maritime trade contacts with the Roman empire. These three dynasties were in constant struggle with each other vying for hegemony over the land. Invasion by the Kalabhras during the 3rd century disturbed the traditional order of the land, displacing the three ruling kingdoms. These occupiers were overthrown by the resurgence of the Pandyas and the Pallavas, who restored the traditional kingdoms. The

Cholas, who re-emerged from obscurity in the 9th century by defeating the Pallavas and the Pandyas, rose to become a great power and extended their empire over the entire southern peninsula. At its height the Chola empire spanned almost 3,600,000 km^2 (1,389,968 sq mi) straddling the Bay of Bengal. The Chola navy held sway over the Sri Vijaya kingdom in Southeast Asia.

A temple from the Chola period. The Cholas united most of the south Indianpeninsula under a single administration during the 10th and the 11th century CE.

Rapid changes in the political situation of the rest of India occurred due to incursions of Muslim armies from the northwest and the decline of the three ancient dynasties during the 14th century, the Tamil country became part of the Vijayanagara Empire. Under this empire, the Kannada speaking Nayak governors ruled before the European trading companiesappeared during the 17th century eventually assuming greater sway over the indigenous rulers of the land. The Madras Presidency, comprising most of southern India, was created in the 18th century and was ruled directly by the British. After the independence of India, after the Telugu and Malayalam parts of Madras state were separated from tamilakam state in 1956, it was renamed as Tamil Nadu in 1969 by the state government.

PRE-HISTORIC PERIOD

Palaeolithic

For most of the Lower Palaeolithic stage, pre-modern humans lived close to river valleys with sparse forest cover or in grassland environments. The population density was very low and so far only two localities of this lower Palaeolithic culture have been found in south India. Pre-modern humans in South India, belonging to the species of *Homo erectus*, lived in this primitive 'old stone age' (Palaeolithic) for quite a long time, using only crude implements such as hand axesand choppers and subsisting as hunter-gatherers.

A discovery of a rare fossilized baby brain in Viluppuram district, by a team of archaeologists was reported in April 2003, It is estimated to be about 187,000 years - 200,000 years or older. The ancestor of modern humans (*Homo sapiens*) who appeared around 50,000 years ago was more developed and could make thinner flake tools and blade-like tools using a variety of stones. From about 10,000 years ago, humans made still smaller tools called Microlithic tools. The material used by the early humans to make these tools were jasper, agate, flint, quartz, etc. In 1949, researchers found such microliths in Tirunelveli district. Archaeological evidence suggests that the microlithic period lasted between 6000–3000 BCE.

Neolithic

In Tamil Nadu, the Neolithic period had its advent around 2500 BCE. Humans of the Neolithic period made their stone tools in finer shapes by grinding and polishing. A Neolithic axe head with ancient writing on it has been found in Tamil Nadu. The Neolithic humans lived mostly on small flat hills or on the foothills in small, more or less permanent settlements but for periodical migration for grazing purposes. They gave the dead proper burials within urns or pits. They were also starting to use copper for making certain tools or weapons.

Iron Age

During the Iron Age humans started using iron for making tools and weapons. The Iron Age culture in peninsular India is marked by Megalithic burial sites, which are found in several hundreds of places. On the bases of both some excavations and the typology of the burial monuments, it has been suggested that there was a gradual spread of the Iron Age sites from the north to the south. Comparative excavations carried out in Adichanallur in Thirunelveli district and in Northern India have provided evidence of a southward migration of the Megalithic culture.

The earliest clear evidence of the presence of the megalithic urn burials are those dating from around 1000 BCE, which have been discovered at various places in Tamil Nadu, notably at Adichanallur, 24 km from Tirunelveli, where archaeologists from the Archaeological Survey of India unearthed 157 urns, including 15 containing human skulls, skeletons and bones, plus husks, grains of rice, charred rice and Neolithic Celts. One urn has writing inside, which, according to archaeologists from the Archaeological Survey of India, resembles early Tamil-Brahmi script, confirming it of the Neolithic period 2800 years ago. Adhichanallur has been announced as an archaeological site for further excavation and studies.

Mentions of the political situation of Tamil Nadu before the common era are found in Ashoka's edicts dated c 300 BCE and, vaguely, in the Hathigumpha inscriptiondated c.150 BCE. The earliest epigraphical evidence in the Tamil country are that of the Pandya king Kadungon (c. 560–590 CE) who displaced the Kalabhras from the Pandyas country. —Nilakanta Sastri, *A history of South India*, pp 105, 137

Early history

Ancient Tamil Nadu contained three monarchical states, headed by kings called *Vendhar* and several tribal chieftaincies, headed by the chiefs called by the general denomination *Vel* or *Velir*. Still lower at the local level there were clan chiefs called *kizhar* or *mannar*. During the 3rd century BCE, the Deccan was part of the Maurya Empire, and from the middle of the 1st century BCE to 2nd century CE the same area was ruled by the Satavahana dynasty. The Tamil area had an independent existence outside the control of these northern empires. The Tamil kings and chiefs were always in conflict with each other mostly over property. The royal courts were mostly places of social gathering rather than places of dispensation of authority; they were centres for distribution of resources.Tamil literature Tolkappiyam sheds some light on early religion. Gradually the rulers came under the influence of Vedic beliefs, which encouraged performance of sacrifices to enhance the status of the ruler. Buddhism, Jainism and Ajivika co-existed with early Shaivite, Vaishnavismand Shaktism during the first five centuries.

The names of the three dynasties, Cholas, Pandyas, and Cheras, are mentioned in the Pillars of Ashoka (inscribed 273–232 BCE) inscriptions, among the kingdoms, which though not subject to Ashoka, were on friendly terms with him. The king of Kalinga, Kharavela, who ruled around 150 BCE, mentioned in the famous Hathigumpha inscription of the confederacy of the Tamil kingdoms that had existed for over 100 years.

Karikala Chola was the most famous early Chola. He is mentioned in a number of poems in the Sangam poetry. In later times Karikala was the subject of many legends found in the *Cilappatikaram* and in inscriptions and literary works of the 11th and 12th centuries. They attribute to him the conquest of the whole of India up to the Himalayas and the construction of the flood banks of the river Kaveri with the aid of his feudatories. These legends however are conspicuous by their absence in the Sangam poetry. Kocengannan was another famous early Chola king who has been extolled in a number of poems of the Sangam period. He was even made a Saiva saint during the medieval period.

Pandyas ruled initially from Korkai, a sea port on the southernmost tip of the Indian peninsula, and in later times moved to Madurai. Pandyas are also mentioned in Sangam Literature, as well as by Greek and Roman sources during this period. Megasthenes in his *Indika* mentions the Pandyan kingdom.

The Pandyas controlled the present districts of Madurai, Tirunelveli, and parts of south Kerala. They had trading contacts with Greece and Rome. With the other kingdoms of Tamilakam, they maintained trading contacts and marital relationships with Tamil merchants from Eelam. Various Pandya kings find mention in a number of poems in the Sangam literature. Among them Nedunjeliyan, 'the victor of Talaiyalanganam' deserves a special mention. Besides several short poems found in the *Akananuru* and the *Purananuru* collections, there are two major works—*Mathuraikkanci* and the *Netunalvatai* (in the collection of *Pattupattu*) that give a glimpse into the society and commercial activities in the Pandyan kingdom during the Sangam age. The early Pandyas went into obscurity at the end of the 3rd century CE during the incursion of the Kalabhras.

The kingdom of the Cheras comprised the modern Western Tamil Nadu and Kerala, along the western or Malabar Coast of southern India. Their proximity to the sea favoured trade with Africa. Chera rulers dated to the first few centuries AD. It records the names of the kings, the princes, and the court poets who extolled them.

The internal chronology of this literature is still far from settled, and at present a connected account of the history of the period cannot be derived. Uthiyan Cheralathan, Nedum Cheralathan and Senguttuvan Chera are some of the rulers referred to in the Sangam poems. Senguttuvan Chera, the most celebrated Chera king, is famous for the legends surrounding Kannagi, the heroine of the Tamil epic *Silapathikaram*. The people of the regions which constitutes the ancient territories of the Cheras spoke Tamil language and had extensive interaction with the rest of the Tamil country. It was only towards the 9th or the 10th centuries CE, due to Sanskrit influences on Tamil, a new language Malayalam began to evolve in western parts of the territory.

These early kingdoms sponsored the growth of some of the oldest extant literature in Tamil. The classical Tamil literature, referred to as Sangam literature is attributed to the period between 200 BCE and 300 CE. The poems of Sangam literature, which deal with emotional and material topics, were categorised and collected into various anthologies during the medieval period. These Sangam poems paint the picture of a fertile land and of a people who were organised into various occupational groups. The governance of the land was through hereditary monarchies, although the sphere of the state's activities and the extent of the ruler's powers were limited through the adherence to the established order (*dharma*). The people were loyal to their kings and roving bards and musicians and danseuse gathered at the royal courts of the generous kings. The arts of music and dancing were highly developed and popular. Musical instruments of various types find mention in the Sangam poems. The amalgamation of the southern and the northern styles of dancing started during this period and is reflected fully in the epic *Cilappatikaram*.

Internal and external trade was well organised and active. Evidence from both archaeology and literature speaks of a flourishing foreign trade with the *Yavanas*(Greeks). The port city of Puhar on the east coast and Muziris on the west coast of south India were emporia of foreign trade, where huge ships moored, offloading precious merchandise. This trade started to decline after the 2nd century CE and the direct contact between the Roman empire and the ancient Tamil country was replaced by trade with the Arabs and the Auxumites of East Africa. Internal trade was also brisk and goods were sold and bartered. Agriculture was the main profession of a vast majority of the populace.

Interregnum (300–700)

After the close of the Sangam era, from about 300 to about 600 CE, there is an almost total lack of information regarding occurrences in the Tamil land. Some time about 300 CE, the whole region was upset by the appearance of the Kalabhras.

These people are described in later literature as 'evil rulers' who overthrew the established Tamil kings and got a strangle hold of the country. Information about their origin and details about their reign is scarce. They did not leave many artefacts or monuments. The only source of information on them is the scattered mentions in Buddhist and Jain literature.

Historians speculate that these people followed Buddhist or Jain faiths and were antagonistic towards the Hindu religions (*viz.* the Astika schools) adhered by the majority of inhabitants of the Tamil region during the early centuries CE. As a result, Hindu scholars and authors who followed their decline in the 7th and 8th century may have expunged any mention of them in their texts and generally tended to paint their rule in a negative light. It is perhaps due to this reason, the period of their rule is known as a 'Dark Age'—an interregnum. Some of the ruling families migrated northwards and found enclaves for themselves away from the Kalabhras. Jainismand Buddhism, took deep roots in the society, giving birth to a large body of ethical poetry.

Writing became very widespread and *vatteluttu* evolved from the Tamil-Brahmi became a mature script for writing Tamil. While several anthologies were compiled by collecting bardic poems of earlier centuries, some of the epic poems such as the *Cilappatikaram* and didactic works such as the *Tirukkural* were also written during this period. The patronage of the Jain and Buddhist scholars by the Kalabhra kings influenced the nature of the literature of the period, and most of the works that can be attributed to this period were written by the Jain and Buddhist authors.

In the field of dance and music, the elite started patronising new polished styles, partly influenced by northern ideas, in the place of the folk styles. A few of the earliest rock-cut temples belong to this period. Brick temples (known as *kottam*, *devakulam*, and *palli*) dedicated to various deities are referred to in literary works. Kalabhras were displaced around the 7th century by the revival of Pallava and Pandya power.

Even with the exit of the Kalabhras, the Jain and Buddhist influence still remained in Tamil Nadu. The early Pandya and the Pallava kings were followers of these faiths. The Hindu reaction to this apparent decline of their religion was growing and reached its peak during the later part of the 7th century. There was a widespread Hindu revival during which a huge body of Saiva and Vaishnava literature was created. Many Saiva Nayanmars and Vaishnava Alvars provided a great stimulus to the growth of popular devotional literature. Karaikkal Ammaiyar who lived in the 6th century CE was the earliest of these Nayanmars. The celebrated Saiva hymnists Sundaramurthi, Thirugnana Sambanthar and Thirunavukkarasar were of this period. Vaishnava Alvars such as Poigai Alvar, Bhoothathalvar and Peyalvar produced devotional hymns for their faith and their songs were collected later into the four thousand poems of *Naalayira Divyap Prabhandham*.

Age of empires (600–1300)

The medieval period of the history of the Tamil country saw the rise and fall of many kingdoms, some of whom went on to the extent of empires, exerting influences both in India and overseas. The Cholas who were very active during the Sangam age were entirely absent during the first few centuries. The period started with the rivalry between the Pandyas and the Pallavas, which in turn caused the revival of the Cholas. The Cholas went on to becoming a great power. Their decline saw the brief resurgence of the Pandyas. This period was also that of the re-invigorated Hinduism during which temple building and religious literature were at their best.

The Hindu sects Saivism and Vaishnavism became dominant, replacing the prevalence of Jainism and Buddhism of the previous era. Saivism was patronised more by the Chola kings and became more or less a state religion. Some of the earliest temples that are still standing were built during this period by the Pallavas. The rock-cut temples in Mamallapuram and the majestic Kailasanatha and Vaikuntaperumal temples of Kanchipuram stand testament to the Pallava art. The Cholas, utilising their prodigious wealth earned through their extensive conquests, built long-lasting stone temples including the great Brihadisvara temple of Thanjavur and exquisite bronze sculptures. Temples dedicated to Siva and Vishnu received liberal donations of money, jewels, animals, and land, and thereby became powerful economic institutions.

Tamil script replaced the *vatteluttu* script throughout Tamil Nadu for writing Tamil. Religious literature flourished during the period. The Tamil epic, Kamban's*Ramavatharam*, was written in the 13th century. A contemporary of Kamban was the famous poet Auvaiyar who found great happiness in writing for young children. The secular literature was mostly court poetry devoted to the eulogy of the rulers. The religious poems of the previous period and the classical literature of the Sangam period were collected and systematised into several anthologies. Sanskrit was patronised by the priestly groups for religious rituals and other ceremonial purposes. Nambi Andar Nambi, who was a contemporary of Rajaraja Chola I, collected and arranged the books on Saivism into eleven books called *Tirumurais*. The hagiology of Saivism was standardised in *Periyapuranam* by Sekkilar, who lived during the reign of Kulothunga Chola II (1133–1150 CE). Jayamkondar's *Kalingattupparani*, a semi-historical account on the two invasions of Kalinga by Kulothunga Chola I was an early example of a biographical work.

Pallavas

The 7th century Tamil Nadu saw the rise of the Pallavas under Mahendravarman I and his son *Mamalla*Narasimhavarman I. The Pallavas were not a recognised political power before the 2nd century. It has been widely accepted by scholars that they were originally executive officers under the Satavahana kings. After the fall of the Satavahanas, they began to get control over parts of Andhra and the Tamil country. Later they had marital ties with the Vishnukundina who ruled over the Deccan. It was around 550

CE under King Simhavishnu that the Pallavas emerged into prominence.

Shore Temple in Mamallapuram built by the Pallavas. (c. eighth century CE)

They subjugated the Cholas and reigned as far south as the Kaveri River. The Pallavas were at their finest during the reigns of Narasimhavarman I and *Pallavamalla* Nandivarman II. Pallavas ruled a large portion of South Indiawith Kanchipuram as their capital. Dravidian architecture during the Pallava rule includes the Shore Temple, built for Narasimhavarman II, which is a UNESCO World Heritage Site. Many sources describe Bodhidharma, the founder of the Zen school of Buddhism in China, as a prince of the Pallava dynasty.

During the 6th and the 7th centuries, the western Deccan saw the rise of the Chalukyas based in Vatapi. Pulakeshin II(c.610–642) invaded the Pallava kingdom in the reign of Mahendravarman I. Narasimhavarman who succeeded Mahendravarman mounted a counter invasion of the Chalukya country and captured the Chalukyan capital Vatapi and ruled it for 12 years. The rivalry between the Chalukyas and the Pallavas continued for another 100 years until the demise of the Chalukyas around 750. The Chalukyas and Pallavas fought numerous battles and the Pallava capital Kanchipuram was occupied by Vikramaditya II during the reign of Nandivarman II. Nandivarman II had a very long reign (732–796). He led an expedition to the Ganga kingdom (south Mysore) in 760. Pallavas were also in constant conflict with the Pandyas and their frontier shifted along the river Kaveri. The Pallavas had the more difficult existence of the two as they had to fight on two fronts—against the Pandyas as wells as the Chalukyas.

Pandyas

Pandya Kadungon (560–590) is credited with the overthrow of the Kalabhras in the south. Kadungon and his son Maravarman Avanisulamani revived the Pandya power. Pandya Cendan extended their rule to the Chera country. His son Arikesari Parantaka Maravarman (c. 650–700) had a long and prosperous rule. He fought many battles and extended the Pandya power. *Pandya* was well known since ancient times, with contacts, even diplomatic, reaching the Roman Empire; during the 13th century, Marco Polomentioned it as the richest empire in existence.

The Pandyan Empire was large enough to pose a serious threat to the Pallava power. Pandya Maravarman Rajasimha aligned with the Chalukya Vikramaditya II and attacked the Pallava king Nandivarman II. Varagunan I defeated the Pallavas in a battle on the banks of the Kaveri. The Pallava king Nandivarman sought to restrain the growing power of the Pandyas and went into an alliance with the feudal chieftains of Kongu and Chera countries. The armies met in several battles and the Pandya forces scored decisive victories in them. Pandyas under Srimara Srivallaba also invaded Sri Lanka and devastated the northern provinces in 840.

The Pandya power continued to grow under Srimara and

encroached further into the Pallava territories. The Pallavas were now facing a new threat in the form of the Rashtrakutas who had replaced the Chalukyas in the western Deccan. However the Pallavas found an able monarch in Nandivarman III, who with the help of his Ganga and Chola allies defeated Srimara at the battle of Tellaru. The Pallava kingdom again extended up to the river Vaigai. The Pandyas suffered further defeats in the hands of the Pallava Nripatunga at Arisil (c. 848). From then the Pandyas had to accept the overlordship of the Pallavas.

Cholas

Around 850, out of obscurity rose Vijayalaya, made use of an opportunity arising out of a conflict between Pandyas and Pallavas, captured Thanjavur from Mutharaiyardynasty and eventually established the imperial line of the medieval Cholas. Vijayalaya revived the Chola dynasty and his son Aditya I helped establish their independence. He invaded Pallava kingdom in 903 and killed the Pallava king Aparajita in battle, ending the Pallava reign. The Chola kingdom under Parantaka Iexpanded to cover the entire Pandya country. However towards the end of his reign he suffered several reverses by the Rashtrakutas who had extended their territories well into the Chola kingdom.

The Cholas went into a temporary decline during the next few years due to weak kings, palace intrigues and succession disputes. Despite a number of attempts the Pandya country could not be completely subdued and the Rashtrakutas were still a powerful enemy in the north. However, the Chola revival began with the accession of Rajaraja Chola I in 985. Cholas rose as a notable military, economic and cultural power in Asia under Rajaraja and his son Rajendra Chola I. The Chola territories stretched from the islands of Maldives in the south to as far north as the banks of the river Ganges in Bengal. Rajaraja Chola conquered peninsular South India, annexed parts of Sri Lanka and occupied the islands of Maldives. Rajendra Chola extended the Chola conquests to the Malayan archipelago by defeating the Srivijayakingdom. He defeated Mahipala, the king of Bihar and Bengal, and to commemorate his victory he built a new capital called Gangaikonda Cholapuram (*the town of Cholas who conquered the Ganges*). At its peak the Chola Empire extended from the island of Sri Lanka in the south to the Godavari basin in the north.

Brihadishwara Temple

The kingdoms along the east coast of India up to the river Ganges acknowledged Chola suzerainty. Chola navies invaded and conquered Srivijaya in the Malayan archipelago. Chola armies exacted tribute from Thailand and the Khmer kingdom of Cambodia. During the reign of Rajaraja and Rajendra, the administration of the Chola empire matured considerably. The empire was divided into a number of self-governing local government units, and the officials were selected through a system of popular elections.

Throughout this period, the Cholas were constantly troubled by the ever resilient Sinhalas trying to overthrow the Chola occupation of Lanka, Pandya princes trying to win independence for their traditional territories, and by the growing ambitions of the Chalukyas in the western Deccan. The history of this period was one of constant warfare between the Cholas and of these antagonists. A balance of power existed between the Chalukyas and the Cholas and there was a tacit acceptance of the Tungabhadra river as the boundary between the two empires. However, the bone of contention between these two powers was the growing Chola influence in the Vengi kingdom. The Cholas and Chalukyas fought many battles and both kingdoms were exhausted by the endless battles and a stalemate existed.

Marital and political alliances between the Eastern Chalukya kings based around Vengi located on the south banks of the river Godavari began during the reign of Rajaraja following his invasion of Vengi. Virarajendra Chola's son Athirajendra Chola was assassinated in a civil disturbance in 1070 and Kulothunga Chola I ascended the Chola throne starting the Chalukya Choladynasty. Kulothunga was a son of the Vengi king Rajaraja Narendra. The Chalukya Chola dynasty saw very capable rulers in Kulothunga Chola I and Vikrama Chola, however the eventual decline of the Chola power practically started during this period. The Cholas lost control of the island of Lanka and were driven out by the revival of Sinhala power. Around 1118 they also lost the control of Vengi to Western Chalukya king Vikramaditya VI and Gangavadi (southern Mysore districts) to the growing power of Hoysala Vishnuvardhana, a Chalukya feudatory. In the Pandya territories, the lack of a controlling central administration caused a number of claimants to the Pandya throne to cause a civil war in which the Sinhalas and the Cholas were involved by proxy. During the last century of the Chola existence, a permanent Hoysala army was stationed in Kanchipuram to protect them from the growing influence of the Pandyas. Rajendra Chola III was the last Chola king.

The Kadava chieftain Kopperunchinga I even captured Rajendra and held him prisoner. At the close of Rajendra's reign (1279), the Pandyan Empire was at the height of prosperity and had completely absorbed the Chola kingdom. The Cholas also found a place in very famous novel by Kalki title Ponniyin Selvan which portrays the whole Chola history with Rajaraja Cholan (Ponniyin Selvan, Arul Mozhi Varman,Vallavarayan Vanthiyaththevan,Karikalar,Nandhini,Kundhavi) as the characters of the novel.

Cheras

The Cheras were an ancient Dravidian royal dynasty of Tamil origin who ruled in regions of Tamil Nadu and Kerala in India.Together with the Chola and the Pandyas, it formed the three principal warring Iron Age kingdoms of southern India in the early centuries of the Common Era. over a wide area comprising Venad, Kuttanad, Kudanad, Pazhinad, and more.

In other words, they governed the area between Alappuzha in the south to Kasargod in the north. This included Palghat, Coimbatore, Salem and Kollimalai. The capital was Vanchi, which the Romans who actively traded with the Cheras knew as Muzris.

By the early centuries of the Common Era, civil society and statehood under the Cheras were developed in present-day western Tamil Nadu. The location of the Chera capital is generally assumed to be at modern Karur (identified with the Korura of Ptolemy). The Chera kingdom later extended to the plains of Kerala, the Palghat gap, along the river Perar and occupied land between the river Perar and river Periyar, creating two harbour towns, Tondi (Tyndis) and Muciri (Muziris), where the Roman trade settlements flourished.

The Cheras were in continuous conflict with the neighbouring Cholas and Pandyas. The Cheras are said to have defeated the combined armies of the Pandyas and the Cholas and their ally states. They also made battles with the Kadambâs of Banavasi and the Yavanas (the Greeks) on the Indian coast. After the 2nd century AD, the Cheras' power decayed rapidly with the decline of the lucrative trade with the Romans.

The Tamil poetic collection called Sangam literature describes a long line of Chera rulers dated to the first few centuries AD. It records the names of the kings, the princes, and the court poets who extolled them. The internal chronology of this literature is still far from settled, and at present a connected account of the history of the period cannot be derived. Uthiyan Cheralathan, Nedum Cheralathan and Senguttuvan Chera are some of the rulers referred to in the Sangam poems. Senguttuvan Chera, the most celebrated Chera king, is famous for the legends surrounding Kannagi, the heroine of the Tamil epic Silapathikaram.

The Chera kingdom owed its importance to trade with West Asia, Greece and Rome. Its geographical advantages, like the abundance of exotic spices, the navigability of the rivers connecting the Ghat mountains with the Arabian sea, and the discovery of favourable Monsoon winds which carried sailing ships directly from the Arabian coast to Chera kingdom, combined to produce a veritable boom in the Chera foreign trade.

The Later Cheras ruled from the 9th century. Little is known about the Cheras between the two dynasties. The second dynasty, Kulasekharas ruled from a city on the banks of River Periyar called Mahodayapuram (Kodungallur). Though never regained the old status in the Peninsula, Kulasekharas fought numerous wars with their powerful neighbors and diminished to history in the 12th century as a result of continuous Chola and Rashtrakuta invasions. The Chera dynasty was supported by Tamil warriors such as Villavar, Vanavar and Malayar clans.

The Chera rulers of Venadu, based at the port Quilon in

southern Kerala, trace their relations back to the later/second Cheras. Ravi Varma Kulasekhara, ruler of Venadu from 1299 to 1314, is known for his ambitious military campaigns to former Pandya and Chola territories.

Pandya revival

After being overshadowed by the Pallavas and Cholas for centuries, the Pandiyas revived their fortunes in the 13th century and the Pandya power extended from the Telugu territories along the banks of the Godavari river to the northern half of Sri Lanka. When Kulasekara Pandyan I died in 1308, a conflict stemming from succession disputes arose amongst his sons – the legitimate Sundara Pandya and the illegitimate Vira Pandya (who was favoured by the king) fought each other for the throne. Soon Madurai fell into the hands of the invading armies of the Delhi Sultanate (which initially gave protection to the vanquished Sundara Pandyan).

Delhi Sultanate

Malik Kafur, a general of the Delhi Sultan Alauddin Khalji invaded and sacked Madurai in 1311. Pandyas and their descendants were confined to a small region around Thirunelveli for a few more years. Ravivarman Kulasekara (r. 1299–1314), a Chera (Perumal) feudatory of Kulasekara Pandya, staked his claim to the Pandya throne. Ravivarman, utilising the unsettled nature of the country, quickly overran the southern Tamil Nadu and brought the entire region from Kanyakumari to Kanchipuram, under the Chera kingdom. His inscription was found in Punaamalli, a suburb of Madras. But, Ravivarman's hold over Kânci was only short-lived and his aggressive activities were arrested by the Kâkatiya ruler, Pratâparudra II. The Kâkatiya army under the command of Muppidi Nâyaka marched to Kanci, and captured the city.

2

Culture and Society

TAMIL CULTURE

Tamil culture is the culture of the Tamil people. Tamil culture is rooted in the arts and ways of life of Tamils in India, Sri Lanka, Malaysia, Singapore and across the globe. Tamil culture is expressed in language, literature, music, dance, theatre, folk arts, martial arts, painting, sculpture, architecture, sports, media, comedy, cuisine, costumes, celebrations, philosophy, religions, traditions, rituals, organizations, science, and technology.

Language and literature

Tamils have strong attachment to the Tamil language, which is often venerated in literature as "*Tamil2ān2n̄2āi* ", "the Tamil mother". It has historically been, and to large extent still is, central to the Tamil identity. Like the other languages of South India, it is a Dravidian language, unrelated to the Indo-European languages of northern India. The Tamil language preserves many features of Proto-Dravidian, though modern-day spoken Tamil in Tamil Nadu freely uses loanwords from Sanskrit and English and vice versa. Tamil literature is of considerable antiquity, and is recognised as a classical language by the government of India. Classical Tamil literature, which ranges from lyric poetry to works on poetics and ethical philosophy, is remarkably different from contemporary and later literature in other Indian languages, and represents the oldest body of secular literature in South-east Asia.

Agathiar, First Sangam period poet of Tamil literature.

Religion

Ancient Tamil grammatical works Tolkappiyam, the ten anthologies Pattuppâmṁu, the eight anthologies Emmūttokai sheds light on early religion of ancient Dravidian people. *Murugan* was glorified as, *the god of war, who is ever young and resplendent,* as *the favored god of the Tamils.* Sivan was also seen as the supreme God. Early iconography of Murugan and Sivan and their association with native flora and fauna goes back to Indus Valley Civilization. The Sangam landscape was classified into five categories, *thinais*, based on the mood, the season and the land. Tolkappiyam, mentions that each of these *thinai* had an associated deity such Seyyon in *Kurinji*-the hills, Thirumaal in *Mullai*-the forests, and Venthan in *Marutham*-the plains, Kotravai in *Palai*-the deesert and Wanji-ko/kadalon in the *Neithal*-the coasts and the seas. Other gods mentioned were Mayyon and Vaali who were all assimilated into Hinduism over time. Dravidian influence on early Vedic religion is evident, many of these features are already present in the oldest known Indo-Aryan language, the language of the *Rigveda* (c. 1500 BCE), which also includes over a dozen words borrowed from Dravidian. This represents an early religious and cultural fusion or synthesisbetween ancient Dravidians and Indo-Aryans, which became more evident over time with sacred iconography, flora and fauna that went on to influence Hinduism, Buddhism and Jainism

About 88% of the population of Tamil Nadu are Hindus. Christians and Muslims account for 6% and 5.5% respectively.The majority of Muslims in Tamil Nadu speak Tamil, with less than 15% of them reporting Urdu as their mother tongue.Tamil Jains number only a few thousand now. Atheist, rationalist, and humanist philosophies are also adhered by sizeable minorities, as a result of Tamil cultural revivalism in the 20th century, and its antipathy to what it saw as Brahminical Hinduism.

The most popular deity is Murugan, he is known as the patron god of the Tamils and is also called "Tamil Kadavul" (Tamil God). In Tamil tradition, Murugan is the youngest son and Ganesha/Pillayar is the eldest son of Shiva/Sivan, and it is different from the North Indian tradition, which represents Murugan as the eldest son. The goddess Parvati is often depicted as a goddess with green skin complexion in Tamil Hindu tradition. The worship of Amman, also called Mariamman, is thought to have been derived from an ancient mother goddess, is also very common. Kan2n2agi, the heroine of the Cilappatikâr, is worshipped as Pattin2i by many Tamils, particularly in Sri Lanka.There are also many followers of Ayyavazhi in Tamil Nadu, mainly in the southern districts. In addition, there are many temples and devotees of Vishnu, Siva,

Ganapathi, and the other Hindu deities. Muslims across Tamil Nadu follow Hanafi and Shafi'i schools. Most Tamil Muslims are Shadhilis. Erwadi in Ramanathapuram district and Nagore in Nagapattinam district are the major pilgrimage centres for Muslims in Tamil Nadu.

The most important Tamil festivals are Pongal, a harvest festival that occurs in mid-January, and Varudapirappu, the Tamil New Year, which occurs on 14 April. Both are celebrated by almost all Tamils, regardless of religion. The Hindu festival Deepavali is celebrated with fanfare; other local Hindu festivals include Thaipusam, Panguni Uttiram, and Adiperukku. While Adiperukku is celebrated with more pomp in the Cauvery region than in others, the Ayyavazhi Festival, Ayya Vaikunda Avataram, is predominantly celebrated in the southern districts of Kanyakumari District, Tirunelveli, and Thoothukudi.

In rural Tamil Nadu, many local deities, called aiyyanârs, are thought to be the spirits of local heroes who protect the village from harm. Their worship often centres around nadukkal, stones erected in memory of heroes who died in battle. This form of worship is mentioned frequently in classical literature and appears to be the surviving remnants of an ancient Tamil tradition.

The Saivist sect of Hinduism is significantly represented amongst Tamils, more so among Sri Lankan Tamils, although most of the Saivist places of religious significance are in northern India. The Alvars and Nayanars, who were predominantly Tamils, played a key role in the renaissance of Bhakti tradition in India. In the 10th century, the philosopher Ramanuja, who propagated the theory of Visishtadvaitam, brought many changes to worshiping practices, creating new regulations on temple worship, and accepted lower-caste Hindus as his prime disciples.

Tamil Jains constitute around 0.13% of the population of Tamil Nadu. Many of the rich Tamil literature works were written by Jains. According to George L. Hart, the legend of the Tamil Sangams or "literary assemblies: was based on the Jain *sangham* at Madurai.

MARTIAL TRADITIONS

Various martial arts including Kuttu Varisai, Varma Kalai, Silambam, Adithada, Malyutham and Kalarippayattu, are practised in Tamil Nadu and Kerala. The warm-up phase includes yoga, meditation and breathing exercises. Silambam originated in ancient Tamilakam and was patronized by the Pandyans, Cholas and Cheras, who ruled over this region. *Silapathiharam* a Tamil literature from the 2nd century AD, refers to the sale of Silamabam instructions, weapons and equipment to foreign traders. Since the early Sangam age, there was a warlike culture in South India. War was regarded as an honorable sacrifice and fallen heroes and kings were worshiped in the form of a Hero stone. Each warrior was trained in martial arts, horse riding and specialized in two of the weapons of that period Vel (spear) Val (sword) and Vil (bow). Heroic martyrdom was glorified in ancient Tamil literature. The Tamil kings and warriors followed an honour code similar to that of Japanese Samuraisand committed suicide to save the honor. The forms of martial suicide were known as Avipalli, Thannai, Verttal, Marakkanchi, Vatakkiruttal and Punkilithu Mudiyum Maram. Avipalli was mentioned in all the works except *Veera Soliyam*. It was a self-sacrifice of a warrior to the goddess of war for the victory of his commander. The Tamil rebels in Sri Lanka reflected some elements of Tamil martial traditions which included worship of fallen heroes (Maaveerar Naal) and practice of martial suicide. They carried a Suicide pill around their neck to escape the captivity and torture. A remarkable feature besides to their willingness to sacrifice is, that they were well organized and disciplined. It was forbidden for the rebels to consume tobaccos, alcohols, drugs and to have sexual relationship.

The Wootz steel originated in South India and Sri Lanka. There are several ancient Tamil, Greek, Chinese and Roman literary references to high carbon Indian steel since the time of Alexander's India campaign. The crucible steel production process started in the sixth century BC, at production sites of Kodumanal in Tamil Nadu, Golconda in Andhra Pradesh,

Karnataka and Sri Lanka and exported globally; the Tamils of the Chera Dynasty producing what was termed *the finest steel in the world*, i.e. Seric Iron to the Romans, Egyptians, Chinese and Arabs by 500 BC. The steel was exported as cakes of steely iron that came to be known as "Wootz."

The Tamilakam method was to heat black magnetite ore in the presence of carbon in a sealed clay crucible inside a charcoal furnace.

An alternative was to smelt the ore first to give wrought iron, then heated and hammered to be rid of slag. The carbon source was bamboo and leaves from plants such as Avârai.

The Chinese and locals in Sri Lanka adopted the production methods of creating Wootz steel from the Chera Tamils by the 5th century BC. In Sri Lanka, this early steel-making method employed a unique wind furnace, driven by the monsoon winds, capable of producing high-carbon steel and production sites from antiquity have emerged, in places such as Anuradhapura, Tissamaharama and Samanalawewa, as well as imported artifacts of ancient iron and steel from Kodumanal.

A 200 BC Tamil trade guild in Tissamaharama, in the South East of Sri Lanka, brought with them some of the oldest iron and steel artifacts and production processes to the island from the classical period.

The Arabs introduced the South Indian/Sri Lankan wootz steel to Damascus, where an industry developed for making weapons of this steel. The 12th century Arab traveler Edrisi mentioned the "Hinduwani" or Indian steel as the best in the world. Another sign of its reputation is seen in a Persian phrase – to give an "Indian answer", meaning "a cut with an Indian sword." Wootz steel was widely exported and traded throughout ancient Europe and the Arab world, and became particularly famous in the Middle East.

Traditional Weapons

The Tamil martial arts also includes various types of weapons.

- Valari (throwing iron sickle)
- Maduvu (deer horns)
- Surul Vaal (curling blade)
- Vaal (sword) + Ketayam (shield)
- Itti or Vel (spear)
- Savuku (whip)
- Kattari (fist blade)
- Veecharuval (battle Machete)
- Silambam (long bamboo staff)
- Kuttu Katai (spiked knuckleduster)
- Katti (dagger/knife)
- Vil (bow)
- Tantayutam (mace)
- Soolam (trident)
- Theekutchi (flaming baton)
- Yeratthai Mulangkol (dual stick)
- Yeretthai Vaal (dual sword)

VISUAL ART AND ARCHITECTURE

Most traditional art are religious in some form and usually centres on Hinduism, although the religious element is often only a means to represent universal—and, occasionally, humanist—themes.

The most important form of Tamil painting is Tanjore painting, which originated in Thanjavur in the 9th century. The painting's base is made of cloth and coated with zinc oxide, over which the image is painted using dyes; it is then decorated with semi-precious stones, as well as silver or gold thread.

A style which is related in origin, but which exhibits significant differences in execution, is used for painting muralson temple walls; the most notable example are the murals on the Kutal Azhakar and Meenakshi templesof Madurai, the Brihadeeswarar temple of Tanjore.

Dancing Siva or Nataraja, example of Chola Empire bronze.

Tamil sculpture ranges from elegant stone sculptures in temples, to bronze icons with exquisite details.The medieval Chola bronzes are considered to be one of India's greatest contributions to the world art. Unlike most Western art, the material in Tamil sculpture does not influence the form taken by the sculpture; instead, the artist imposes his/her vision of the form on the material. As a result, one often sees in stone sculptures flowing forms that are usually reserved for metal.

MUSIC

Tamil country has its own music form called Tamil Pannisai, from which current carnatic music evolved. Has its own music troops like Urumi melam, Pandi melam (present day's chenda melam), Mangala Vathiyam, Kailaya vathiyam etc.,. Ancient Tamil works, such as the *Silappatikaram*, describe a system of music, and a 7th-century Pallava inscription at Kudimiyamalai contains one of the earliest surviving examples of Indian music in notation. Contemporary dance forms such as Bharatanatyam have recent origins but are based older temple dance forms known as *Sadirattam* as practised by courtesans and a class of women known as *Devadasis*

Performing arts

Famous Tamil dance styles are

- Bharatanatyam (Tamil classical dance)
- Sadirattam (Tamil classical dance- erotic music and movements similar to mohiniattam)
- Karakattam (Tamil ancient folk dance)
- Koothu (A folk and street dance)
- Kaliyal (A folk dance using sticks and intricate movements)
- Devarattam (A dance of warriors)
- Kai-silambam (A folk dance holding silambam in hand)
- Paraiattam (A folk drums and dance)
- Kavadiattam (dedicated to the Tamil God Murugan)
- Kummiyattam (female folk dance)
- Bommalattam (Puppet dance)
- Puliyattam (Tiger dance)
- Mayilattam (Peacock dance)
- Paampu attam (snake dance)
- Oyilattam (Dance of Grace)
- Poikkaal Kuthirai Aattam (False legged horses dance)

Contemporary dance forms such as Bharatanatyam have recent origins but are based older temple dance forms known as *Catir Kacceri* as practised by courtesans and a class of women known as *Devadasis* One of the Tamil folk dances is *karakattam*. In its religious form, the dance is performed in front of an image of the goddess Mariamma. The *kuravanci* is a type of dance-drama, performed by four to eight women. The drama is opened by a woman playing the part of a female soothsayer of the *kurava* tribe(people of hills and mountains), who tells the story of a lady pining for her lover.

The therukoothu, literally meaning "street play", is a form of village theater or folk opera. It is traditionally performed in village squares, with no sets and very simple props. The performances involve songs and dances, and the stories can be either religious or secular. The performances are not formal, and performers often interact with the audience, mocking them, or involving them in the dialogue.

Therukkûthu has, in recent times, been very successfully adapted to convey social messages, such as abstinence and anti-caste criticism, as well as information about legal rights, and has spread to other parts of India. Tamil Nadu also has a well developed stage theatre tradition, which has been influenced by western theatre. A number of theatrical companies exist, with repertoires including absurdist, realist, and humorous plays.

FILM AND THEATER ARTS

The theatrical culture that flourished Tamil culture during the classical age. Tamil theatre has a long and varied history whose origins can be traced back almost two millennia to dance-theatre forms like *Kotukotti* and *Pandarangam*, which are mentioned in an ancient anthology of poems entitled the *Kalingathu Parani.*

The predominant theater form of the region is Kattaikkuttu, where performers (historically men) sing, act, dance and are accompanied by musicians on traditional instruments. The majority of performances draw from stories in the Mahabharata, while a few plays take their inspiration from Purana stories.

The modern Tamil film industry originated during the 20th century. Tamil film industry has its headquarters in Chennai and is known under the name Kollywood, it is the second largest film industry in India after Bollywood. Films from Kollywood entertain audiences not only in India but also overseas Tamil diaspora.

Tamil films from Chennai have been distributed to various overseas theatres in Singapore, Sri Lanka, South Africa, Malaysia, Japan, Oceania, the Middle East, Western Europe, and North America.

Inspired by Kollywood originated outside India Independent Tamil film production in Sri Lanka, Singapore, Canada, and western Europe. Several Tamil actresses such as Anuisa Ranjan Vyjayanthimala, Hema Malini, Rekha Ganesan, Sridevi, Meenakshi Sheshadri, and Vidya Balan have acted in Bollywood and dominated the cinema over the years. Some Chief Ministers of Tamil Nadu like MG Ramachandran, Karunanidhi and Jayalalithaa have their background in Tamil film industry.

Jallikattu

In Ancient times, two bullfighting and bull-racing sports were conducted. 1.Manjuvirattu and 2. Yeruthazhuval. These sports were organised to keep the people's temperament always fit and ready for the war at any time. Each has its own techniques and rules. These sports acted as one of the criteria to marry girls of warrior family. There were traditions where the winner would be chosen as bridegroom for their daughter or sister.

Mr. Gandhirajan, who is a post-graduate in Art History from Madurai-Kamaraj University, said the ancient Tamil tradition was "manju virattu" (chasing bulls) or "eruthu kattuthal" (lassoing bulls) and it was never "jallikattu," that is baiting a bull or controlling it as the custom obtained today. In ancient Tamil country, during the harvest festival, decorated bulls would be let loose on the "peru vazhi" (highway) and the village youth would take pride in chasing them and outrunning them. Women, elders and children would watch the fun from the sidelines of the "peru vazhi" or streets. Nobody was injured in this. Or the village youth would take delight in lassoing the sprinting bulls with "vadam" (rope).

It was about 500 years ago, after the advent of the Nayak rule in Tamil Nadu with its Telugu rulers and chieftains, that this harmless bull-chasing sport metamorphosed into "jallikattu," said Mr. Gandhirajan.

The ancient Tamil art of unarmed bullfighting, popular amongst warriors in the classical period, has also survived in parts of Tamil Nadu, notably Alanganallurnear Madurai, where it is known as Jallikattu and is held once a year around the time of the Pongal festival.

3

Government and Politics

GOVERNMENT OF TAMIL NADU

Fort St George, Chief Secretariat, Govt of Tamil Nadu

The Government of Tamil Nadu is the governing authority for the Indian state of Tamil Nadu. It is seated at Fort St

George, Chennai. The legislature of Tamil Nadu was bicameral until 1986, when it was replaced by a unicameral legislature, like most other states in India.

Structure

The Governor is the constitutional head of state while the Chief Minister heads the council of ministers. The Chief Justiceof the Madras High Court is the *head of the judiciary*.

Officials

Presently Banwarilal Purohit is the governor and Edappadi K.Palanisamy is the Chief Minister of Tamil Nadu. Vijaya Kamlesh Tahilramani is the current Chief Justice of Madras High Court.

Administrative divisions

The state of Tamil Nadu has a population of 7,21,38,959 as per the 2011 Census and covers an area of 1,30,058 km^2. The major administrative units of the state constitute 32 districts, 76 revenue divisions, 220 taluks, 12 municipal corporations, 148 municipalities, 385 panchayat unions (blocks), 561 town panchayats and 12,524 village panchayats.

E-governance

The Tamil Nadu E-Governance Agency is the entity that facilitates e-governance efforts in Tamil Nadu.

As part of the e-governance initiative, a large part of government records like land ownership records have been digitised. All major administrative offices like local governance bodies and various government departments have been computerised.

TAMIL NADU LEGISLATURE

The Tamil Nadu Legislature is the unicameral legislature of the Indian state of Tamil Nadu. The Legislature is composed of Tamil Nadu Legislative Assembly and the Governor of Tamil Nadu

Until 1986, the Tamil Nadu Legislature was a bicameral legislature consisting of:

- the Tamil Nadu Legislative Assembly, the lower house,
- the Tamil Nadu Legislative Council, the upper house, and
- the Governor of Tamil Nadu

In 2010, the erstwhile Dravida Munnetra Kazhagam (DMK) Government took steps to revive the Tamil Nadu Legislative Council and convert the legislature back into a bicameral one, but the administration left power during this time and was unable to continue. The present All India Anna Dravida Munnetra Kazhagam (AIADMK) Government has expressed its intent not to revive the Tamil Nadu Legislative Council.

ELECTIONS IN TAMIL NADU

Elections in Tamil Nadu are conducted every five years to elect the State assembly and its share of members to the Lok Sabha. There are 234 assembly constituencies and 39 Lok Sabha constituencies. The state has conducted 15 assembly elections and 16 Lok Sabha elections since independence.

Assembly constituencies

Tamil Nadu has 234 assembly constituencies. The Chief Minister of the state is elected by legislators of the political party or coalition commanding an assembly majority, and serves a five-year term with a provision of re-election.

The Governor is the head of state, but his or her role is largely ceremonial.

The Lok Sabha is the directly elected lower house of the Parliament of India. As of 2014 there have been sixteen Lok Sabhas elected by the people of India. Tamil Nadu has 39 Lok Sabha constituencies.

POLITICS OF TAMIL NADU

Politics of Tamil Nadu is the politics related to the Indian state of Tamil Nadu.

History of Tamil Nadu politics

Pre-Dravidian politics of Tamil Nadu

Indian National Congress dominated the political scene in the initial years post independence with leaders like C. Rajagopalachari and K. Kamaraj. The political influence shifted from national politics towards regional politics with rise of Dravida Munnetra Kazhagam in the late 1960s.

Rise of Dravidian politics

Dravidian parties have dominated state politics since 1967. One of the earliest regional parties was the South Indian Welfare Association, which was founded in 1916. It came to be known as the Justice Party after the name of its English-language daily, *Justice*. E.V. Ramasami, popularly known as "Periyar", renamed the party Dravidar Kazhagam in 1944. DK was a non-political party which demanded the establishment of an independent state called Dravida Nadu. However, due to the differences between its two leaders Periyar and C.N. Annadurai, the party was split. Annadurai left the party to form the Dravida Munnetra Kazhagam (DMK). The DMK decided to enter into politics in 1956.

The Anti-Hindi agitations in the mid-1960s made the DMK more popular and more powerful political force in the state. The DMK routed the Indian National Congressparty in the 1967 elections and took control of the state government, ending Congress's stronghold in Tamil Nadu.

C.N. Annadurai became the DMK's first Chief Minister, and Muthuvel Karunanidhi took over as Chief Minister and party leader after Annadurai's death in 1969.Karunanidhi's leadership was soon challenged by M.G. Ramachandran, popularly known as MGR.

In 1972, he split from DMK and formed the All India Anna Dravida Munnetra Kazhagam (AIADMK). He was the Chief Minister of the state from 1977 until his death in 1987. After the death of MGR, the party split again into two factions, one led by Janaki Ramachandran, wife of MGR, and the other led by J. Jayalalithaa. After the defeat of AIADMK in 1989 assembly polls, both factions were merged and Jayalalithaa took control of the party. She was elected as the General Secretary of the unified AIADMK. There have been splits in both the DMK and the AIADMK, but since 1967 one of those two parties has held power in the state. In the State elections after M.G. Ramachandran's death, neither of the two parties could come back to power in consecutive assembly elections. Governments were formed by: DMK in 1989, AIADMK in 1991, DMK alliance in 1996, AIADMK alliance in 2001, DMK alliance in 2006 and AIADMK alliance consecutively in 2011 and 2016.

Tamil Nationalism in politics

Tamil Nationalism has been part of the Tamil political Arena ever since a Tamil identity pride has been created among the Tamil populace in the late 19th century. Dravidian movement and Tamil nationalism rose from the same roots. They differed in very few but important topics, such as eradication casteism , promoting religious equality and extermination of untouchability. While Dravidian parties take these topics at the same level of Promotion of Tamil, the Tamil organizations sole priority was promotion of Tamil. On multiple occasions they were religious and sometimes refused to acknowledge the caste problems.

During the Anti Hindi Imposition Movement, the Tamil Nationalist organizations converged with Dravidian parties on the common ground of Protecting and Promoting Tamil. In the next oncoming decades, the relevance of the Tamil Nationalist Parties reduced to a great degree. Still many Tamil Nationalist organizations keep on working on promotion of Tamil identity.

Such parties and their policies can be classified into a wider spectrum. There are organization which claim every person with an intent to promote Tamil identity as a Tamil. At the same time, few elements classify and deny Tamil identity to the people of Tamil Nadu based on Caste lines, which is in total contrast to the former type.

After the death of Velupillai Prabhakaran, a revival, even though not a big enough to create an impact in political balance, is seen. The success of this new wave is yet to be seen.

Political culture of Tamil Nadu

Freebie Culture

Politics in Tamil Nadu has had a strongly socialist character since the rise of Dravidian politics in the 1960s. In Tamil Nadu, DMK and AIADMK are alternately elected by people in Tamil Nadu and a strong third party does not exist. Both DMK and AIADMK, the major political parties in Tamil Nadu, as per their political and economic policy, made sure that the people of the state receive the fruits of the modern technology. Whichever party was in the rule, made sure that all the households have a television set, the womenfolk have access to work on the economy of their family by providing them household appliances and the students have all the necessary tools to reach and complete their education namely bicycle, textbooks, stationery and laptops.

At the same time, the promise of and distribution of freebies is considered and criticized to be a form of bribery, disguised as people welfare. The right wing political parties and economists feel that the fiscal profligacy and handouts don't make economic sense and, importantly, they tend to make people lazy. The leftists and the left leaning parties have raised concerns about the revenue model used for financing the freebie schemes. They accuse the two parties of *depoliticizing* the electorate and bribing the voters to turn blind eye to the corruptions of the regimes These social welfare schemes provide the Dravidian faction of the Tamilnadu politics an edge over the other regional and national parties.

Caste Politics

Tamil Nadu has seen numerous caste based parties, serving two purposes. Either to represent the genuine concerns of the oppressed communities or to create Votebanks for ruling parties.

The Dalit political parties, representing the oppressed societies have been fighting for social justice. Typically reservation in education and job opportunities are demanded by such parties. In Tamil Nadu such parties are also supporters of Tamil Nationalism. Rarely some of the parties have claimed that the castes they represent are oppressed by being declared a part of the Scheduled castes list. They demand removal of their caste from Scheduled castes list and to rename their caste.

However, people from the relatively upper castes and also have founded political parties. They fear that their opportunities are robbed by the concessions extended to the SC and ST communities. They have demanded to get their castes declare as backward to avail reservation.

The effect of the caste politics is debatable and could not be expected end in near future. In 2001, the sitting DMK government came up with a huge a alliance with caste parties and was defeated in 2001 assembly election. Still caste based political parties are part of both the ruling and opposition alliances in all the successive elections.

Celebrity worship

Many people from the Tamil film industry are active in Tamil Nadu politics. Some of the Chief Ministers of Tamil Nadu like MG Ramachandran, Karunanidhi and Jayalalithaa have their background in the Tamil film industry. The worship of party leader by members is widely spread in Tamil Nadu, sometimes it reaches a fanatical level. This worship culture originates during the era of MGR.

The youngsters were often a factor that changes the dynamic of Tamil Nadu politics, what can be seen in Anti-Hindi agitations of Tamil Nadu, 2013 Anti–Sri Lanka protests and 2017 pro-jallikattu protests.

DRAVIDIAN PARTIES

Dravidian parties include an array of regional political parties in the state of Tamil Nadu, India, which trace their origins and ideologies either directly or indirectly to the Dravidian movement of Periyar E. V. Ramasamy. The Dravidian movement was based on the linguistic divide in India, where most of the Northern Indian, Eastern Indian and Western Indian languages are classified as Indo-Aryan, whereas the South Indian languages are classified as Dravidian. Dravidian politics has developed by associating itself to the Dravidian community. The original goal of Dravidian politics was to achieve social equality, but it later championed the cause of ending the domination of North India over the politics and economy of the South Indian province known as Madras Presidency.

Most Dravidian parties are offshoots of Dravidar Kazhagam (DK). There are also a few other parties in Tamil Nadu that did not arise from DK directly. Nevertheless, both the former and the latter are considered as Dravidian parties because of the similarities of their ideals and goals. Dravida Munnetra Kazhagam (DMK) and its political rival Anna Dravida Munnetra Kazhagam (AIADMK) have been the major players among the Dravidian parties since the mid-1960s. Since the 1967 legislative assembly elections, only the DMK and the AIADMK have formed governments in Tamil Nadu. These two parties are political rivals. Barring political alliances with the DMK or AIADMK, since the 1990s no other political party has won more than a few seats in the Indian parliament or state legislative assembly of Tamil Nadu. Since 1996, members of the DMK and AIADMK have held portfolios in the cabinet of the central Indian government.Another Dravidian party is Marumalarchi Dravida Munnetra Kazhagam.

Political media is pervasive in Dravidian politics, with five of the seven chief ministers from these parties being directly involved in Tamil cinema, either as script writers or actors. Recently television channels owned by these parties have been used for political propaganda purposes.

Rise of Dravidian politics

Most of the Indian population are classified as Aryans and Dravidians. Based on language families. Most northern Indian languages are classified as Aryan, whereas most southern Indian languages are Dravidian languages.

The term Aryan as a race was first propounded by the German employee of East India Company, Fredrich Maxmillan Muller aka Max Muller who in 1853 proposed that a group of people called Aryans had invaded India in 1500 BC. This theory was actively supported by the British colonialists of the period led by Thomas Macaulay who stated that there was a need to develop a breed of Indian "who would be Indian by blood and colour but Western by morals and intellect". Sanskrit, a classical language of the Aryan group, was considered to be a sacred language, whereas in the former British Indian state of Madras Presidency, it was a commonly held opinion in that the Dravidian tongues were inferior.

The linguistic divide was even more pronounced given the political dominance of Brahmins in South India. The Brahmins, who occupied the highest strata in the Indian caste system, accounted for 3% of the population in Madras Presidency, but held 60 to 79% of the positions in major government departments in the early 20th century. It was observed by some non-Brahmin leaders from the south that Brahmins were Aryans, and hence non-natives, who had taken positions in the government that should rightfully be filled by people indigenous to the area. The antipathy towards Sanskrit compounded with the animosity against the Brahimins paved the way for the rise of Dravidian politics in Madras Presidency.

Early Dravidian politics

An early pioneer in Dravidian politics was Iyothee Thass in the late 19th century. His efforts brought together the lower caste Dravidians with the establishment of the *Dravida Mahajana Sabha* organisation in 1891.

A major leap in Dravidian politics was the formation of the *Madras United League* by non-Brahmin intellectuals, who considered the dominance of Brahmins in civil administration a threat to the non-Brahmin majority. The League was initially started as a workgroup that helped non-Brahmin students in

Madras with accommodation. It later grew into a political party under the efforts of leaders like Sir Pitti Theagaroya Chetty and Dr. T. M. Nair. The party was named *South Indian Liberal Federation (S. I. L. F.)* – popularly known as the Justice party.

Justice Party era

A limited form of self governance was introduced in British India after World War I. While the Justice Party saw this as an opportunity to displace Brahmin dominance, the British government considered it favourable, since the Indian National Congress spearheading the Indian independence movement was dominated by Brahmins. The Justice party emerged as a winner in the 1920 general elections and brought about the reforms it had campaigned for, including establishing communal reservation through affirmative action for the first time in the country, and brought temples under state control. Soon after their electoral success the animosity between Tamil and Telugu members deepened, thus weakening the party. Nevertheless, the Justice Party electorally dominated the presidency for 17 years until it was defeated by the Indian National Congress party in 1937. Although out of power, the Justice Party was involved in demonstrations across the Province against the introduction of Hindi as a compulsory subject of study in schools by a Congress-led government, which led to the detainment of scores of Tamil scholars, academics and Justice Party leaders. This and other struggles for social justice helped create the social base of what emerged as the Dravidian Movement.

Dravidar Kazhagam

The next few years saw a decline in the Justice Party's popularity. In 1938, the by then badly weakened party sought the leadership of Periyar E. V. Ramasamy, a leader of the Dravidian Movement, who became its president. In 1944, Periyar changed the name of the party to Dravidar Kazhagam (Dravidian organisation" in English). This move was opposed by some members of the Party who continued contesting elections as the Justice Party under the leadership of P. T.

Rajan until 1957. Periyar as the president of Dravidiar Kazhagam considered that contesting in elections would lead to compromises in principles and withdrew Dravida Kazhagam from parliamentary politics.

Dravida Munnetra Kazhagam

Birth of DMK

In 1947, when India attained independence, Periyar called for members of the Dravidar Kazhagam to boycott the celebrations. According to him, the Indian National Congress was dominated by Brahmins. He predicted that an independent India would bring South Indians, especially Tamils, under the dominance of Brahmins and North Indians. In other words, according to Periyar, independence would lead to the replacement of British dominance with Brahmin and North Indian dominance. He felt an independent nation called Dravida Nadu for the South Indians would be the best solution. Periyar declared 15 August 1947, the day of Indian independence, as a day of mourning. This move was opposed by other leaders within the party, including C. N. Annadurai. Annadurai viewed independence as an achievement for all of India rather than solely of the Aryan North. On 9 July 1948 Periyar married woman 40 years his junior, leading to a split in the party. The leaders of the splitting faction eventually formed a new party, Dravida Munnetra Kazhagam or DMK (Progressive Dravidian Organisation in English), in 1949.

Independent Dravida Nadu

Although initially both DK and DMK sought an independent Dravida Nadu, DK later moved on to work on bringing social changes whereas DMK leaders such as C. N. Annadurai and E. V. K. Sampath endeavoured to achieve their goals through parliamentary election processes. Sampath, who had earlier forfeited his seniority with Periyar's party to join DMK, saw the call for an independent Dravida Nadu was turning out to be an unrealistic goal. Sampath expressed concerns over using film stars to increase the popularity of the party. His views led him to cross swords with the major leaders of the party and eventually caused the first split in DMK. Sampath left DMK to begin his own party called the Tamil National Party. Although leaders like Annadurai were firm in their separatist stance, the reorganisation of states in India on a linguistic basis removed Kannada, Telugu and Malayalam speaking regions from Madras Presidency, leaving behind a predominantly Tamil Madras State. Giving in to political realities, Annadurai and his DMK changed their call for an independent *Dravida Nadu for Dravidians* to an independent *Tamil Nadu for Tamils*. Annadurai saw that remaining in the Indian Union meant accepting linguistic domination and economic backwardness. However, the Sino-Indian war brought about changes in the Indian constitution. The Sixteenth Amendment (also known as the *Anti-Secessionist Amendment*) banned any party with sectarian principles from contesting elections. Consequently, DMK preferred to keep the issue of Dravida Nadu on the backburner. From then on DMK's main focus targeted the dominance of North Indians in the Union Government of India.

DMK government

After dropping the demand for an independent Dravida Nadu, DMK changed its focus to the problems arising out of the disparity between North and South India. The DMK considered that the south was neglected by delays in sanctioning development projects and allotment of funds. Thus the Congress-led Central government became its major target for calls for reform. Immediately after Indian independence the Congress Party was popular throughout India and thus formed the government in many states including Madras Presidency. Even so, the Congress Party failed to obtain an absolute majority in the presidency in the state's first election. By the 1960s the popularity of the Congress party was in a steady decline.

DMK leaders also perceived that the attempts to declare Hindi as the sole national language of India was an attempt impose an Aryan language unwilling people in the South.

According to the terms of the Indian constitution dated 26 January 1965, English as an official language of India would come to an end and Hindi would become the sole official language. However, the Madras Anti-Hindi agitation in 1965 compelled the Central Government in India change its language policy, allowing English to continue as an official language. Although DMK was not directly involved in the violence that marred the agitation, the protest itself catapulted DMK to political power in the State in the 1967 legislative elections. Annadurai became the first non-Congress Chief Minister of the post-1950 Madras state as a result.

The electoral victory in 1967 led to an electoral fusion among the non-Congress parties to avoid a split in the Opposition votes. Rajagopalachari, a former senior leader of the Congress Party, had by then left the Congress and launched the right-wing Swatantra Party. He played a vital role in bringing about the electoral fusion amongst the opposition parties to align against the Congress.

Split in DMK and birth of AIADMK

MGR and the split from DMK

M. G. Ramachandran, popularly known as MGR, was an actor in Tamil cinema and a well known propagator of Dravidian ideologies in his movies since 1953. In the 1970s as the then treasurer of DMK, he played a vital part in popularising the party, bringing many of his fans as supporters.

A political feud between MGR and the party's president M. Karunanidhi had been ongoing since the death of Annadurai in 1969. It arose from Karunanidhi calling himself the "Mujib of Tamil Nadu". Soon after the electoral victory of DMK in 1971, some of senior members expressed concern that MGR's popularity was growing strong within the party cadres.

Karunanidhi made several attempts to weaken MGR's position within the party. MGR retaliated with corruption charges and a call for a boycott of the party's General Council. DMK's General Council suspended MGR from the party stating that he had involved himself in "anti party activities". Although

MGR had lost support from top-ranking leaders within the DMK, the strong public reaction following his suspension demonstrated his popular support within the party's volunteers. Inspired by this support from the party's lower cadres and his fans, MGR launched his own party, Anna Dravida Munnetra Kazhagam (AIADMK, Anna DMK named after Annadurai: Anna was his nickname).

AIADMK government

MGR presented his new party to Indira Gandhi as the regional equivalent of her Congress (I) Party. Indira Gandhi was the head of her party, which she split from the Indian National Congress with the support of lower cadres and opposition from senior party leaders. Thus AIADMK could show itself as an equally strong alternative to that of DMK with which Congress (I) could ally. From then on, the Congress (I) Party fought elections in the State in alliance with one of the two parties. Ever since then the Dravidian parties have helped the Congress (I) sustain itself in the State, but with limited ambitions.

In 1977, the DMK government, led by Karunanidhi, was dismissed under corruption charges by the Central government of India, led by Congress (I), which had by then allied with AIADMK.

Further divisions

Further offshoots of DMK

Sivaji Ganesan, a veteran actor of Tamil Cinema, was a founding member of DMK party. The actor himself was nicknamed Sivaji by Periyar E. V. Ramasami after his role portraying the Maratha king. Nevertheless, differences between the party leadership and the actor widened since he perceived that M. G. Ramachandran, his acting contemporary, was given more prominence than himself. Furthermore, he started distancing himself from the party's anti-religious atheistic stance to satisfy his religious fans. Hence when E. V. K. Sampath launched his own splinter from DMK (in the name of Tamil National Party), Sivaji left DMK and joined Sampath. However, Tamil National Party itself was short-lived and was merged into Congress. Sivaji, although a member of Congress party, maintained distance from the party activities and concentrated more on his film career. After the death of M. G. Ramachandran in 1987, Sivaji re-launched his political career with his own party Thamizhaga Munnetra Munnani ("Tamil Nadu Development Front" in English). The party lost every single seat it contested for in the 1989 elections. Sivaji dissolved the party, asked his party cadres to join the Janata Dal and openly regretted his decision to have ever launched his own party.

The Marumalarchi Dravida Munnetra Kazhagam ("Progressive Dravidian Renaissance Organisation" in English, or MDMK) is yet another offshoot of the DMK. It was formed in May 1994, after V. Gopalswamy (popularly known as Vaiko), a senior leader and Member of Parliament from DMK, was expelled from the party. Barring, perhaps, their more radical support for an independent Tamil Eelam in the Sri Lankan crisis, the MDMK do not have major ideological differences with the other Dravidian parties. MDMK shares its goals with the DMK and AIADMK in respect to State autonomy, constitutional protection for the reservation formula and making Tamil an official language of the Indian Union. In 2004, Tamil film director and actor T. Rajendar who was earlier expelled from DMK launched the All India Latchiya Dravida Munnetra Kazhagam ("All India Principled Dravida Munnetra Kazhagam" in English).

Offshoots of AIADMK

Soon after MGR's death in 1987, his wife Janaki Ramachandran took over as Chief Minister of Tamil Nadu. This appointment was opposed by former actress and politician J. Jayalalithaa. The resistance from Jayalalithaa eventually led to the dismissal of the AIADMK government, the shortest lived government in the history of Tamil Nadu, by the Central

Government of India then led by Rajiv Gandhi. The antagonism built up and the AIADMK split into two fragments.

The Election Commission of India refused to accept either of them as the successor of the original party and separate electoral symbols were allocated. The faction led by MGR's widow chose to use *two doves*, with a large dove holding leafy branch in its beak, as if feeding the smaller dove. Jayalalithaa's faction was represented by a *crowing cock*. Although both factions lost the 1989 state elections, Jayalalithaa's AIADMK won 27 seats when compared to just one won by Janaki's.Following the election defeat, Janaki retired from active politics and the two party factions rejoined into one party.

Other breakaways in AIADMK were witnessed in 1990s, when R. M. Veerappan and S. Tirunavukkarasu, due to personal differences with Jayalalithaa, formed MGR Kazhagam (MGR's Organisation) and MGR ADMK (MGR's and Anna's DMK) respectively.

Dravidian parties in central government

Although the DMK and the AIADMK started playing a minimal role in the decision-making process in the Central government in the late 1960s, their actual participation in coalition governments came only in 1979, when two AIADMK Members of Parliament, Satyavani Muthu and Aravinda Bala Pajanor, joined the short-lived Charan Singh Ministry, which followed the Morarji Desai-led Janata Party government (1977–79). The DMK's Murasoli Maran joined the V.P. Singh Ministry in 1989. The DMK shared power with the subsequent United Front governments led by H.D. Deve Gowda and I.K. Gujral. In the Atal Bihari Vajpayee Ministry (1998–99), three parties from Tamil Nadu, the AIADMK, the Marumalarchi Dravida Munnetra Kazhagam (MDMK) and the Pattali Makkal Katchi (PMK) were represented. In the BJP-led National Democratic Alliance (NDA) Ministry, headed by Vajpayee (1999–2004), the DMK, the MDMK and the PMK all had representatives. In fact, it was in this Ministry that Tamil Nadu had the largest representation. At one stage there were 10 Ministers from Tamil Nadu, seven of them from the Dravidian parties. In the Vajpayee Ministry (1998–99), the AIADMK's presence lasted only a few months. The Manmohan Singh-led central government included cabinet members from DMK.

Ideology

Dravidianism and Tamilism

The principal ideals and goals of Dravidian parties at their incipience, which were borrowed from Dravidar Kazhagam, were social reforms such as ending religious beliefs, ending caste distinction, empowerment of women, ending Brahmin dominance in Tamil Nadu educational institutions and government, ending northern domination of the politics and economy of Tamil Nadu, opposition to Hindi as India's official language, and independence for Dravida Nadu from India. The call for Dravida Nadu in the initial days during the British Raj meant a "Dravidian state under the British Raj". Although Annadurai defended his party's demand for Dravida Nadu in his maiden speech in the Rajya Sabha in 1962 and recorded his protest against a ban on demanding separation, a year later the demand had to be abandoned following the Sino-Indian War. This paradigm shift is often attributed to the *Sixteenth Amendment to the Indian Constitution* or *Anti-sectionist* amendment, as it is usually called. In the 1960s, the formation of Tamil Nadu as a Tamil language state carved out of the erstwhile Madras Presidency fulfilled the goal of an encompassing Dravidian state.

Since then, state autonomy and social justice through reservation for the underprivileged in education and employment have been the main political planks of the DMK.

The Dravidian political ideology has evolved through the years and is now varied between parties.

Starting from an initial atheistic inclination with the strict anti-Brahmin outlook of the DK, the DMK moved on to a strong ethnic identity – initially that of "the Dravidian" and later of "the Tamilian" or "the common Tamil man". In fact it is considered that Dravidian politics developed into an inclusive Tamil nationalism since it associated the Dravidian community with the non-Sanskritic Tamil language and cultural tradition.

The AIADMK however, never adopted the anti-Brahmin and anti-Hindu stance of the DK and DMK and opposed exclusion on the lines of ethnicity. After MGR's death, the dispute over whom should head the AIADMK was led by Janaki and Jayalalithaa, who were both Brahmins. The latter is now the head of the AIADMK. One of the four AIADMK Chief Ministers- MGR (a Malayali Nair) was not even Tamilian. But the party's position on other issues such as reservation, Hindi, federalism, Sri Lankan Tamils etc. is common with that of the other Dravidian parties.

Leftist inclination

The Self-respect movement, which is at the root of Dravidian politics, was initially forged in the mid-1920s in emulation and in critique of the Gandhian Congress Party, but by the 1930s it was heavily influenced by Leninist socialism, atheism and Bertrand Russell's inspired rationalism. C. N. Annadurai, the first Chief Minister of Tamil Nadu from the Dravidian parties, declared that the DMK (and hence its offshoots) are "genuinely communist by principle". MGR's AIADMK adopted *Annaism*, a political philosophy which in MGR's own words, was "a proper amalgam of capitalism, socialism and communism".

Political use of media

Mass media have been widely used by Dravidian politicians from the early days of the parties. Initially propaganda was spread through newspapers owned by benefactors or by the organisations themselves and through public gatherings. One early example of media use was the magazine Justice, which carried strong non-Brahmin viewpoints, after which the Indian Justice Party was named. A later example is Kudi Arasu (*The Republic* in English). DMK had Murasoli (*Drum Beat* in English) as its party organ, and AIADMK published Namathu Dr MGR (*Our Dr. MGR* in English). Dinakaran, a Tamil Daily owned by Marans, was earlier considered as an unofficial organ of DMK until the family feud within the family of Karunanidhi.

Tamil cinema and politics

Tamil cinema first became politicized during the Non-cooperation movement. With the advent of sound in films, large numbers of theater personnel were attracted, many of whom were already active in politics. Annadurai was a writer, director, and producer of many films that were used as a means of propagation of Dravidian ideologies.

Sivaji Ganesan was a member of DK but later moved to DMK as one of its founding members. Nevertheless, he was expelled from the DMK following his comments on the party being a "glamour party", a reaction which is attributed to his frustration over lack of recognition.

M. G. Ramachandran was reputedly the most famous star of any Dravidian party. Former Chief Minister of Tamil Nadu Karunanidhi has continued be active both in film script writing and politics until recent times. Former Chief Ministers of Tamil Nadu Janaki Ramachandran and J. Jayalalitha were both film stars who paired with MGR in many of his movies. Other stars within the Dravidian parties include S. S. Rajendran and K. R. Ramaswamy.

Television

DMK initially used Sun TV Network for its propaganda which eventually led to the birth of the alternate Tamil Channel Kalaignar TV. Similarly, AIADMK earlier owned JJ TV, which was later dissolved. It currently uses Jaya TV for its propaganda.

Impact

Regional

One of the major impacts of the Dravidian parties is said to be the lack of or limited support to the Hindutva movement, which swept the Hindi heartlands of India, in Tamil Nadu. The announcement in 1990 by the then Prime Minister V.P. Singh that the Mandal Commission's recommendation to extend reservation in employment in the Union government to the Other Backward Classes would be implemented was "in accordance with the resolution to that effect, passed in the State Assembly" is claimed by DMK to be one of its achievements. Listing the benefits accruing to the State from sharing power at the Centre, the DMK stated that "the presence of the DMK Minister (Murasoli Maran) in the National Front Cabinet and the resolution passed in the (Tamil Nadu) Assembly during the DMK regime (1996–2001) resulted in a Tribunal being appointed to adjudicate the Kaveri River Water Dispute in the case filed by the Thanjavur farmers in the Supreme Court". The success of the efforts of Prime Minister Vajpayee in persuading Karnataka to accept the Tribunal's Interim Award ensuring 205 tmc.ft. of Kaveri river water to Tamil Nadu has been seen as one of the benefits of the DMK's presence in the BJP-led government.

According to the DMK, the "creation" of 11 Navaratnas and 97 Mini-Ratnas companies in the public sector, (blue-chip companies which invest 30 per cent of their surplus funds in public sector mutual funds) "with administrative and financial autonomy", during the United Front government at the Centre (1996–98) was because of the party's presence in the Cabinet.

Another benefit cited by DMK is the substantial profits the State has received from foreign investments since the start of the liberalisation process. According to a party statement, of the total investment of Rs.13,150,170 millions that has flowed into the country since liberalisation began, Tamil Nadu has received 1,511,870 millions, which is 11.5 per cent of the total investment in the country.

It is the DMK chief Karunanidhi who played a vital role in the then central government declaring Tamil a classical language.

National

Between 1996 and 2014, either DMK or AIADMK has been part of the central governments of India. The inclusion of DMK in the United Front government, led by I. K. Gujral, in 1997 came under crisis with the interim report of Jain Commission, which was appointed to oversee the assassination of Rajiv Gandhi, said that the then DMK government was responsible for abetting Rajiv Gandhi's murderers. In 2007 DMK chief Karunanidi sparked controversy with his remarks on Lord Rama, causing political unrest and resulting in the filing of a First Information Report against him.

International

The Dravidian parties have played a pivotal role in the past Sri Lankan civil war. M. G. Ramachandran, then AIADMK chief, is said to have donated 110 million Indian Rupees to the LTTE. It was also reported by the Jain Commission that the DMK regime was aligned with the LTTE between 1989 and 1991. S. Ramadoss, party chief of PMK, has recently called for the Central Government of India to help work towards an "early political solution in Sri Lanka." In 2007 DMK, AIADMK and MDMK expressed their concerns over the arrest of Tamil Malaysians following a protest.

4

Language and Literature

TAMIL LANGUAGE

Tamil is a Dravidian language predominantly spoken by the Tamil people of India and Sri Lanka, and by the Tamil diaspora, Sri Lankan Moors, Burghers, Douglas, and Chindians. Tamil is an official language of three countries: India, Sri Lanka and Singapore.

It has official status in the Indian state of Tamil Nadu and the Indian Union Territory of Puducherry. It is used as one of the languages of education in Malaysia, along with English, Malay and Mandarin. Tamil is spoken by significant minorities in the four other South Indian states of Kerala, Karnataka, Andhra Pradesh and Telangana and the Union Territory of the Andaman and Nicobar Islands. It is one of the 22 scheduled languages of India.

Tamil is one of the longest-surviving classical languages in the world. Tamil-Brahmi inscriptions from 500 BC have been found on Adichanallur and 2,200-year-old Tamil-Brahmi inscriptions have been found on Samanamalai. A. K. Ramanujan described it as "the only language of contemporary India which is recognizably continuous with a classical past." The variety and quality of classical Tamil literature has led to it being described as "one of the great classical traditions and literature of the world".

A recorded Tamil literature has been documented for over 2000 years. The earliest period of Tamil literature, Sangam literature, is dated from ca. 300 BC – AD 300. It has the oldest extant literature among Dravidian languages. The earliest epigraphic records found on rock edicts and 'hero stones' date from around the 3rd century BC. More than 55% of the epigraphical inscriptions (about 55,000) found by the Archaeological Survey of India are in the Tamil language. Tamil language inscriptions written in Brahmi script have been discovered in Sri Lanka and on trade goods in Thailand and Egypt. The two earliest manuscripts from India, acknowledged and registered by the UNESCO Memory of the World register in 1997 and 2005, were written in Tamil.

In 1578, Portuguese Christian missionaries published a Tamil prayer book in old Tamil script named *Thambiraan Vanakkam*, thus making Tamil the first Indian language to be printed and published. The *Tamil Lexicon,* published by the University of Madras, was one of the earliest dictionaries published in the Indian languages. According to a 2001 survey, there were 1,863 newspapers published in Tamil, of which 353 were dailies.

Classification

Tamil belongs to the southern branch of the Dravidian languages, a family of around 26 languages native to the Indian subcontinent. It is also classified as being part of a Tamil language family that, alongside Tamil proper, includes the languages of about 35 ethno-linguistic groups such as the Irula and Yerukula languages.

The closest major relative of Tamil is Malayalam; the two began diverging around the 9th century AD. Although many of the differences between Tamil and Malayalam demonstrate a pre-historic split of the western dialect, the process of separation into a distinct language, Malayalam, was not completed until sometime in the 13th or 14th century.

History

According to linguists like Bhadriraju Krishnamurti, Tamil, as a Dravidian language, descends from Proto-Dravidian, a proto-language. Linguistic reconstruction suggests that Proto-Dravidian was spoken around the third millennium BC, possibly in the region around the lower Godavari river basin in peninsular India. The material evidence suggests that the speakers of Proto-Dravidian were of the culture associated with the Neolithic complexes of South India. The next phase in the reconstructed proto-history of Tamil is Proto-South-Dravidian. The linguistic evidence suggests that Proto-South-Dravidian was spoken around the middle of the second millennium BC, and that proto-Tamil emerged around the 3rd century BC. The earliest epigraphic attestations of Tamil are generally taken to have been written shortly thereafter.

Among Indian languages, Tamil has the most ancient non-Sanskritic Indian literature. Scholars categorise the attested history of the language into three periods: Old Tamil (300 BC–AD 700), Middle Tamil (700–1600) and Modern Tamil (1600–present). In November 2007, an excavation at Quseir-al-Qadim revealed Egyptian pottery dating back to first century BC with ancient Tamil Brahmi inscriptions. John Guy states that Tamil was the lingua franca for early maritime traders from India.

Legend

Ujjain/Sâtavâhana symbol, crescented six-arch chaitya hill and river with Tamil Brahmi script Obv: Bust of king; Prakrit legend in the Brahmiscript

According to Hindu legend, Tamil or in personification form Tamil Thâi (Mother Tamil) was created by Lord Shiva. Murugan, revered as the Tamil God, along with sage Agastya, brought it to the people.

Etymology

The earliest extant Tamil literary works and their commentaries celebrate the Pandiyan Kings for the organization of long-termed Tamil Sangams, which researched, developed and made amendments in Tamil language. Even though the name of the language which was developed by these Tamil Sangams is mentioned as Tamil, the period when the name "Tamil" came to be applied to the language is unclear, as is the precise etymology of the name. The earliest attested use of the name is found in Tholkappiyam, which is dated as early as 1st century BC. Southworth suggests that the name comes from _tam-mi;□_ > _tam-i;□_"self-speak", or "one's own speech". Kamil Zvelebil suggests an etymology of _tam-i;□_, with _tam_ meaning "self" or "one's self", and "_-i;□_" having the connotation of "unfolding sound". Alternatively, he suggests a derivation of _tami;□_ < _tam-i;□_ < _*tav-i;□_ < _*tak-i;□_, meaning in origin "the proper process (of speaking)".

The Tamil Lexicon of University of Madras defines the word "Tamil" as "sweetness". S. V. Subramanian suggests the meaning "sweet sound" from _tam_ — "sweet" and _il_ — "sound".

Old Tamil

Old Tamil is the period of the Tamil language spanning the 3rd century BC to the 8th century AD. The earliest records in Old Tamil are short inscriptions from between the 3rd and 2nd century BC in caves and on pottery. These inscriptions are written in a variant of the Brahmi script called Tamil-Brahmi. The earliest long text in Old Tamil is the _Tolkâppiyam_, an early work on Tamil grammar and poetics, whose oldest layers could be as old as the 1st century BC. A large number of literary works in Old Tamil have also survived. These include a corpus of 2,381 poems collectively known as Sangam literature. These poems are usually dated to between the 1st and 5th centuries AD.

Middle Tamil

The evolution of Old Tamil into Middle Tamil, which is generally taken to have been completed by the 8th century, was characterised by a number of phonological and grammatical changes. In phonological terms, the most important shifts were the virtual disappearance of the aytam ("), an old phoneme, the coalescence of the alveolar and dental nasals, and the transformation of the alveolar plosive into a rhotic. In grammar, the most important change was the emergence of the present tense.

Tamil inscriptions in Vatteluttu script in stone during Chola period c.1000 AD at Brahadeeswara temple in Thanjavur, Tamil Nadu.

The present tense evolved out of the verb *kil* ("), meaning "to be possible" or "to befall". In Old Tamil, this verb was used as an aspect marker to indicate that an action was micro-durative, non-sustained or non-lasting, usually in combination with a time marker such as *I*□ ("). In Middle Tamil, this usage evolved into a present tense marker – *kiI_*□*a* (") – which combined the old aspect and time markers.

Modern Tamil

The Nannul remains the standard normative grammar for modern literary Tamil, which therefore continues to be based on Middle Tamil of the 13th century rather than on Modern Tamil. Colloquial spoken Tamil, in contrast, shows a number of changes. The negative conjugation of verbs, for example, has fallen out of use in Modern Tamil – instead, negation is expressed either morphologically or syntactically. Modern spoken Tamil also shows a number of sound changes, in particular, a tendency to lower high vowels in initial and medial positions, and the disappearance of vowels between plosives and between a plosive and rhotic.

Contact with European languages affected written and spoken Tamil. Changes in written Tamil include the use of European-style punctuation and the use of consonant clusters that were not permitted in Middle Tamil. The syntax of written Tamil has also changed, with the introduction of new aspectual auxiliaries and more complex sentence structures, and with the emergence of a more rigid word order that resembles the syntactic argument structure of English. Simultaneously, a strong strain of linguistic purism emerged in the early 20th century, culminating in the Pure Tamil Movement which called for removal of all Sanskritic elements from Tamil. It received some support from Dravidian parties. This led to the replacement of a significant number of Sanskrit loanwords by Tamil equivalents, though many others remain.

GEOGRAPHIC DISTRIBUTION

Tamil is the primary language of the majority of the people residing in Tamil Nadu, Puducherry, in India and Northern Province, Eastern Province, in Sri Lanka. The language is spoken among small minority groups in other states of India which include Karnataka, Andhra Pradesh, Kerala, Maharashtra and in certain regions of Sri Lanka such as Colombo and the hill country. Tamil or dialects of it were used widely in the state of Kerala as the major language of administration, literature and common usage until the 12th century AD. Tamil was also used widely in inscriptions found in southern Andhra Pradesh districts of Chittoor and Nelloreuntil the 12th century AD. Tamil was used for inscriptions from the 10th through 14th centuries in southern Karnataka districts such as Kolar, Mysore, Mandya and Bangalore.

There are currently sizeable Tamil-speaking populations descended from colonial-era migrants in Malaysia, Singapore, Philippines, Mauritius, South Africa, Indonesia, Thailand, Burma, and Vietnam. A large community of Pakistani Tamilsspeakers exists in Karachi, Pakistan, which includes Tamil-speaking Hindus as well as Christians and Muslims – including some Tamil-speaking Muslim refugees from Sri Lanka. Many in Réunion, Guyana, Fiji, Suriname, and Trinidad and Tobagohave Tamil origins, but only a small number speak the language. In Reunion where the Tamil language was forbidden to be learnt and used in public space by France it is now being relearnt by students and adults. It is also used by groups of migrants from Sri Lanka and India, Canada (especially Toronto), United States (especially New Jersey and New York City), Australia, many Middle Eastern countries, and some European countries.

Legal status

Tamil is the official language of the Indian state of Tamil Nadu and one of the 22 languages under schedule 8 of the constitution of India. It is one of the official languages of the union territory of Puducherry and the Andaman and Nicobar Islands. Tamil is also one of the official languages of Singapore. Tamil is one of the official and national languages of Sri Lanka, along with Sinhala. It was once given nominal official status in the Indian state of Haryana, purportedly as a rebuff to Punjab, though there was no attested Tamil-speaking population in the state, and was later replaced by Punjabi, in 2010. In Malaysia, 543 primary education government schools are available fully in Tamil medium. The establishments of Tamil medium schools have been currently in process in Myanmar to provide education completely in Tamil language by the Tamils who settled there 200 years ago. Tamil is taught in Canada for the local Tamil minority populations and the month of January has been declared "Tamil Heritage Month" by the Parliament of Canada. Tamil enjoys a special status of protection under Article 6(b), Chapter 1 of the Constitution of South Africa and is taught as a subject in schools in KwaZulu-Natal province. Recently, it has been rolled out as a subject of study in schools in the French overseas department of Réunion.

In addition, with the creation in October 2004 of a legal status for classical languages by the Government of India and following a political campaign supported by several Tamil associations, Tamil became the first legally recognised Classical language of India. The recognition was announced by the contemporaneous President of India, Abdul Kalam, in a joint sitting of both houses of the Indian Parliament on 6 June 2004.

Dialects

Region-specific variations

The socio-linguistic situation of Tamil is characterised by diglossia: there are two separate registers varying by socioeconomic status, a high register and a low one. Tamil dialects are primarily differentiated from each other by the fact that they have undergone different phonological changes and sound shifts in evolving from Old Tamil.

Old Tamil's *iE□kaG□* (where *kan□* means place) is the source of *iE□kane* in the dialect of Tirunelveli, Old Tamil *iE□kamm□u* is the source of *iE□kumm□u* in the dialect of Madurai, and *iE□kam□e* in some northern dialects. Even now, in the Coimbatore area, it is common to hear "*akkamm□a*" meaning "that place". Although Tamil dialects do not differ significantly in their vocabulary, there are a few exceptions. The dialects spoken in Sri Lanka retain many words and grammatical forms that are not in everyday use in India, and use many other words slightly differently. Tamil dialects include

Central Tamil dialect, Kongu Tamil, Madras Bashai, Madurai Tamil, Nellai Tamil, Kumari tamil in India and Batticaloa Tamil dialect, Jaffna Tamil dialect, Negombo Tamil dialect in Sri Lanka. Sankethi dialect in Karnataka has been heavily influenced by Kannada.

Loanword variations

The dialect of the district of Palakkad in Kerala has a large number of Malayalam loanwords, has been influenced by Malayalam's syntax, and has a distinctive Malayalam accent. Similarly, Tamil spoken in Kanyakumari District has more unique words and phonetic style than Tamil spoken at other parts of Tamil Nadu. The words and phonetics are so different that a person from Kanyakumari district is easily identifiable by their spoken Tamil. Hebbar and Mandyam dialects, spoken by groups of Tamil Vaishnavites who migrated to Karnataka in the 11th century, retain many features of the *Vaishnava paribasai*, a special form of Tamil developed in the 9th and 10th centuries that reflect Vaishnavite religious and spiritual values. Several castes have their own sociolects which most members of that caste traditionally used regardless of where they come from. It is often possible to identify a person's caste by their speech. Tamil in Sri Lanka incorporates loan words from Portuguese, Dutch, and English.

SPOKEN AND LITERARY VARIANTS

In addition to its dialects, Tamil exhibits different forms: a classical literary style modelled on the ancient language (*sankattami;*□), a modern literary and formal style (*centami;*□), and a modern colloquial form (*kom*□*untami;*□). These styles shade into each other, forming a stylistic continuum. For example, it is possible to write *centami;*□ with a vocabulary drawn from *caE*□*kattami;*□ , or to use forms associated with one of the other variants while speaking *kom*□*untami;*□ .

In modern times, *centami;*□ is generally used in formal writing and speech. For instance, it is the language of textbooks, of much of Tamil literature and of public speaking and debate.

In recent times, however, *kom□untami;□* has been making inroads into areas that have traditionally been considered the province of *centami;□*. Most contemporary cinema, theatre and popular entertainment on television and radio, for example, is in *kom□untami;□* , and many politicians use it to bring themselves closer to their audience. The increasing use of *kom□untami;□* in modern times has led to the emergence of unofficial 'standard' spoken dialects. In India, the 'standard' *kom□untami;□* , rather than on any one dialect, but has been significantly influenced by the dialects of Thanjavur and Madurai. In Sri Lanka, the standard is based on the dialect of Jaffna.

WRITING SYSTEM

After Tamil Brahmi fell out of use, Tamil was written using a script called the *vamm□e;□uttu* amongst others such as Grantha and Pallava script. The current Tamil script consists of 12 vowels, 18 consonants and one special character, the *âytam*. The vowels and consonants combine to form 216 compound characters, giving a total of 247 characters (12 + 18 + 1 + (12 x 18)). All consonants have an inherent vowel *a*, as with other Indic scripts. This inherent vowel is removed by adding a tittle called a *pu77□i* , to the consonantal sign.

In addition to the standard characters, six characters taken from the Grantha script, which was used in the Tamil region to write Sanskrit, are sometimes used to represent sounds not native to Tamil, that is, words adopted from Sanskrit, Prakrit and other languages. The traditional system prescribed by classical grammars for writing loan-words, which involves respelling them in accordance with Tamil phonology, remains, but is not always consistently applied. ISO 15919is an international standard for the transliteration of Tamil and other Indic scripts into Latin characters. It uses diacritics to map the much larger set of Brahmic consonants and vowels to the Latin script. Tamil can be transliterated into English by using ISO 15919, since English language uses the Latin script for writing.

LANGUAGES SPOKEN IN TAMIL NADU

Tamil is the official language of Tamil Nadu state and one of the 18 languages mentioned in the eighth schedule of the Indian constitution. Tamil is one of the classical languages of the world, with a rich heritage of literature. It is the most widely spoken language in Tamil Nadu. Besides Tamil Nadu, Tamil is also spoken by a number of people in Sri Lanka, Singapore, Mauritius and Malaysia. The antiquity of Tamil is comparable to Sanskrit. Tamil is written in a derivative of the southern 'Brahmi' script. The alphabet of Tamil is unique (phonetic). That is, in Tamil language letters represent sounds, rather than ideas, as is the case in the 'Mandarin' language of China.

Tamil is spoken by most of the people while around ten percent of the people residing in Tamil Nadu speak Telugu. Other languages that are popular in the state are Kannada, Urdu and Malayalam (though they are spoken by much smaller percentage). The influence of the Malayalam language is more prominent in the west while people residing mostly in the North Eastern part, bordering Karnataka, speak Kannada. Besides the above-mentioned languages, English is also spoken as a subsidiary language in Tamil Nadu.

TAMIL LANGUAGE

Tamil language, member of the Dravidian language family, spoken primarily in India. It is the official language of the Indian state of Tamil Nadu and the union territory of Puducherry (Pondicherry). It is also an official language in Sri Lanka and Singapore and has significant numbers of speakers in Malaysia, Mauritius, Fiji, and South Africa. In 2004 Tamil was declared a classical language of India, meaning that it met three criteria: its origins are ancient; it has an independent tradition; and it possesses a considerable body of ancient literature. In the early 21st century more than 66 million people were Tamil speakers.

The earliest Tamil writing is attested in inscriptions and potsherds from the 5th century BCE. Three periods have been distinguished through analyses of grammatical and lexical changes: Old Tamil (from about 450 BCE to 700 CE), Middle Tamil (700–1600), and Modern Tamil (from 1600). The Tamil writing system evolved from the Brahmi script. The shape of the letters changed enormously over time, eventually stabilizing when printing was introduced in the 16th century CE. The major addition to the alphabet was the incorporation of Grantha letters to write unassimilated Sanskrit words, although a few letters with irregular shapes were standardized during the modern period. A script known as Vatteluttu ("Round Script") is also in common use.

Spoken Tamil has changed substantially over time, including changes in the phonological structure of words. This has created diglossia—a system in which there are distinct differences between colloquial forms of a language and those that are used in formal and written contexts. The major regional variation is between the form spoken in India and that spoken in Jaffna (Sri Lanka), capital of a former Tamil city-state, and its surrounds. Within Tamil Nadu there are phonological differences between the northern, western, and southern speech. Regional varieties of the language intersect with varieties that are based on social class or caste.

Like the other Dravidian languages, Tamil is characterized by a series of retroflexconsonants (/l/, /G/, and /m/) made by curling the tip of the tongue back to the roof of the mouth. Structurally, Tamil is a verb-final language that allows flexibility regarding the order of the subject and the object in a sentence. Adjectives and relative, adverbial, and infinitive clauses normally precede the term they modify, while inflections such as those for tense, number, person, and case are indicated with suffixes.

TAMIL LITERATURE

Tamil literature refers to the literature in the Tamil language. Tamil literature has a rich and long literary tradition spanning more than two thousand years. The oldest extant works show signs of maturity indicating an even longer period of evolution. Contributors to the Tamil literature are mainly from Tamil people from South India, including the land now comprising Tamil Nadu, Kerala, Sri Lankan Tamils from Sri Lanka, and from Tamil diaspora.

The history of Tamil literature follows the history of Tamil Nadu, closely following the social, political and cultural trends of various periods. The early Sangamliterature, starting from the period of 2nd century BCE (Akananuru (1, 15, 31, 55, 61, 65, 91, 97, 101, 115, 127, 187, 197, 201, 211, 233, 251, 265, 281, 311, 325, 331, 347, 349, 359, 393, 281, 295), Kurunthogai (11), Natrinai (14, 75) are dated before 300 BCE), contain anthologies of various poets dealing with many aspects of life, including love, war, social values and religion. This was followed by the early epics and moral literature, authored by Hindu, Jain and Buddhist authors, lasting up to the 5th century CE. From the 6th to 12th century CE, the Tamil devotional poems written by Nayanmars (sages of Shaivism) and Alvars (sages of Vaishnavism), heralded the great Bhakti movement which later engulfed the entire Indian subcontinent. It is during this era that some of the grandest of Tamil literary classics like Kambaramayanam and Periya Puranam were authored and many poets were patronized by the imperial Chola and Pandya empires. The later medieval period saw many assorted minor literary works and also contributions by a few Muslim and European authors.

A revival of Tamil literature took place from the late 19th century when works of religious and philosophical nature were written in a style that made it easier for the common people to enjoy. The modern Tamil literary movement started with Subramania Bharathi, the multifaceted Indian Nationalist poet and author, and was quickly followed up by many who began to utilize the power of literature in influencing the masses. With growth of literacy, Tamil prose began to blossom and mature. Short stories and novels began to appear. Modern Tamil literary criticism also evolved. The popularity of Tamil cinema has also interacted with Tamil literature in some mutually enriching ways.

Sangam age

Sangam literature comprises some of the oldest extant Tamil literature, and deals with love, traditions, war, governance, trade and bereavement. Unfortunately much of the Tamil literature belonging to the Sangam period has been lost. The literature currently available from this period is perhaps just a fraction of the wealth of material produced during this golden age of Tamil civilization. The available literature from this period has been broadly divided in antiquity into three categories based roughly on chronology. These are: the Eighteen Greater Text Series (*Pathinenmaelkanakku*) comprising the Eight Anthologies (*Ettuthokai*) and the Ten Idylls (*Pattupattu*) and the Five Great Epics. *Tolkaappiyam*, a commentary on grammar, phonetics, rhetoric and poetics is dated from this period.

Tamil legends hold that these were composed in three successive poetic assemblies (*Sangam*) that were held in ancient times on a now vanished continent far to the south of India. A significant amount of literature could have preceded *Tolkappiyam* as grammar books are usually written after the existence of literature over long periods. Tamil tradition holds the earliest *Sangam* poetry to be over twelve millennia old. Modern linguistic scholarship places the poems between the 1st century BC and the 3rd century AD.

Sangam age is considered by the Tamil people as the golden era of Tamil language. This was the period when the Tamil country was ruled by the three 'crowned kings' the Cheras, Pandyas and the Cholas. The land was at peace with no major external threats. Asoka's conquests did not impact on the Tamil land and the people were able to indulge in literary pursuits. The poets had a much more casual relationship with their rulers than can be imagined in later times. They could chide them when they are perceived to wander from the straight and narrow. The greatness of the Sangam age poetry may be ascribed not so much to its antiquity, but due to the fact that their ancestors were indulging in literary pursuits and logical classification of the habitats and society in a systematic manner with little to draw from precedents domestically or elsewhere. The fact that these classifications were documented at a very early date in the grammatical treatise *Tolkappiyam*, demonstrates the organized manner in which the Tamil language has evolved.

Tolkappiyam is not merely a textbook on Tamil grammar giving the inflection and syntax of words and sentences but also includes classification of habitats, animals, plants and human beings. The discussion on human emotions and interactions is particularly significant. Tolkappiyam divided into three chapters: orthography, etymology and subject matter (*Porul*). While the first two chapters of Tolkappiyam help codify the language, the last part, *Porul* refers to the people and their behavior. The grammar helps to convey the literary message on human behavior and conduct, and uniquely merges the language with its people.

The literature was classified into the broad categories of 'subjective' (*akam*) and 'objective' (*puram*) topics to enable the poetic minds to discuss any topic under the sun, from grammar to love, within the framework of well prescribed, socially accepted conventions. Subjective topics refer to the personal or human aspect of emotions that cannot be verbalized adequately or explained fully. It can only be experienced by the individuals and includes love and sexual relationship.

Recognizing that human activities cannot take place in vacuum and are constantly influenced by environmental factors, human experiences, in general, and subjective topics in particular, are assigned to specific habitats. Accordingly, land was classified into five genres (*thinai*): *kurinji* (mountainous regions), *mullai* (forests), *marutham*(agricultural lands), *neithal* (seashore), *paalai* (wasteland). The images associated with these landscapes – birds, beasts, flowers, gods, music, people, weather, seasons – were used to subtly convey a mood, associated with an aspect of life. *Kuruntokai*, a collection of poems belonging to the *Ettuthokai* anthology demonstrates an early treatment of the Sangam landscape. Such treatments are found to be much refined in the later works of *Akananuru* and *Paripaatal*. *Paripaatal* takes its name from the musical *Paripaatal meter* utilised in these poems. This is the first instance of a work set to music. *Akaval* and *kalippa* were the other popular meters used by poets during the Sangam age.

Post-Sangam period

Didactic age

The three centuries after the Sangam age . The invaders replaced number of words and concepts relating to ethics, philosophy and religion of Tamil. As a result, Tamil has around 30% of Sanskrit in today's use. However, today, the Indo-Aryan Migration theory has been debunked as baseless and without concrete evidence.Around 300 CE, the Tamil land was under the influence of a group of people known as the Kalabhras. The Kalabhras were Buddhist and a number of Buddhist authors flourished during this period. Jainism and Buddhism saw rapid growth. These authors, perhaps reflecting the austere nature of their faiths, created works mainly on morality and ethics. A number of Jain and Buddhist poets contributed to the creation of these didactic works as well as grammar and lexicography. The collection the Eighteen Lesser Text series (*Pathinenkilkanakku*) was of this period.

The best known of these works on ethics is the *Tirukkural* by Thiruvalluvar. The book is a comprehensive manual of ethics, polity and love, containing 1,330 distichs or *kural* divided into chapters of ten distichs each: the first thirty-eight on ethics, the next seventy on polity and the remainder on love.

Hindu devotional period

The fall of the Kalabhras around 500 CE saw a reaction from the thus far suppressed Hindus. The Kalabhras were replaced by the Pandyas in the south and by the Pallavas in the north. Even with the exit of the Kalabhras, the Jain and Buddhist influence still remained in Tamil Nadu. The early Pandya and the Pallava kings were followers of these faiths.

The Hindu reaction to this apparent decline of their religion was growing and reached its peak during the later part of the 7th century. There was a widespread Hindu revival during which a huge body of Saiva and Vaishnava literature was created. Many Saiva Nayanmars and Vaishnava Alvars provided a great stimulus to the growth of popular devotional literature. Karaikkal Ammaiyar who lived in the 6th century CE was the earliest of these Nayanmars. The celebrated Saiva hymnists Sundaramoorthy, Thirugnana Sambanthar and Thirunavukkarasar (also known as *Appar*) were of this period. Of Appar's verses 3066 have survived. Sambandar sang 4,169 verses. Together these form the first six books of the Saiva canon, collected by Nambi Andar Nambi in the 10th century. Sundarar wrote *Tiruttondartokai* which gives the list of sixty-two Nayanmars. This was later elaborated by Sekkilar in his *Periyapuranam*(4,272 verses). Manikkavasagar, who lived around the 8th century CE was a minister in the Pandya court. His *Tiruvasakam* consisting of over 600 verses is noted for its passionate devotion.. These Saivite Hymns collectively called Thirumurai is described as SIXTH VEDA next to Bhagavath Geetha in Hindu Tradition.

Along with the Saiva Nayanmars, Vaishnava Alvars were also producing devotional hymns and their songs were collected later into the Four Thousand Sacred Hymns (*Naalayira Divyap Prabhandham*). The three earliest Alvars were Poygai, Pudam and Pey. Each of these wrote one hundred *Venpas*. Tirumalisai Alwar who was a contemporary of the PallavaMahendravarman I wrote such works as *Naanmugantiruvadiandadi*. Tirumangai Alvar who lived in the 8th century CE was a more prolific writer and his works constitute about a third of the Diyaprabhandam. Periyalvar and his adopted daughter Andal contributed nearly 650 hymns to the Vaishnava canon. Andal symbolised purity and love for the God and wrote her hymns addressing Vishnu as a lover. The hymn of Andal which starts with *Vaaranam Aayiram* (One Thousand Elephants) tells of her dream wedding to Vishnu and is sung even today at Tamil Vaishnava weddings. Nammalvar, who lived in the 9th century, wrote *Tiruvaimoli.* It comprises 1,101 stanzas and is held in great esteem for its elucidation of the Upanishads. This corpus was collected by Nathamuni, around 950 CE and formed the classical and vernacular basis for Sri Vaishnavism. These Hymns 'Naalayira Divya-p-Prabhandham' is respected at par with Vedas by Sri Vaishnavites in sanctity and holiness and hence referred to as 'Dravida Vedam'.

Narrative epics

Cilappatikaram is one of the outstanding works of general literature of this period. The authorship and exact date of the classic *Cilappatikaram* are not definitely known. Ilango Adigal, who is credited with this work was reputed to be the brother of the Sangam age Chera king Senguttuvan. However we have no information of such a brother in the numerous poems sung on the Chera king. The *Cilappatikaram* is unique in its vivid portrayal of the ancient Tamil land. This is unknown in other works of this period. *Cilappatikaram* and its companion epic *Manimekalai* are Jain in philosophy. *Manimekalai* was written by Sattanar who was a contemporary of Ilango Adigal. Manimekalai contains a long exposition of fallacies of logic which is considered to be based on the 5th century Sanskrit work *Nyayapravesa* by Dinnag. Kongu Velir, a Jain author wrote *Perunkathai* based on the Sanskrit *Brihat-katha. Valayapathi* and *Kundalakesi* are the names of two other narrative poems of this period written by a Jain and a Buddhist author respectively. These works have been lost and only a few poems of *Valayapathi* have been found so far.

Medieval literature

The medieval period was the period of the Imperial Cholas when the entire south India was under a single administration. The period between the 11th and the 13th centuries, during which the Chola power was at its peak, there were relatively few foreign incursions and the life for the Tamil people was one of peace and prosperity. It also provided the opportunity for the people to interact with cultures beyond their own, as the Cholas ruled over most of the South India, Sri Lanka and traded with the kingdoms in southeast Asia. The Cholas built numerous temples, mainly for their favourite god Siva, and these were celebrated in numerous hymns. The *Prabhanda*became the dominant form of poetry. The religious canons of Saiva and Vaishnava sects were beginning to be systematically collected and categorised.

Nambi Andar Nambi, who was a contemporary of Rajaraja Chola I, collected and arranged the books on Saivism into eleven books called *Tirumurais*. The hagiology of Saivism was standardised in *Periyapuranam* (also known as *Tiruttondar Puranam*) by Sekkilar, who lived during the reign of Kulothunga Chola II (1133–1150 CE). Religious books on the Vaishnava sect were mostly composed in Sanskrit during this period. The great Vaishnava leader Ramanuja lived during the reigns of Athirajendra Chola and Kulothunga Chola I, and had to face religious persecution from the Cholas who belonged to the Saiva sect. One of the best known Tamil works of this period is the *Ramavatharam* by Kamban who flourished during the reign of Kulottunga III. *Ramavatharam* is the greatest epic in Tamil Literature, and although the author states that he followed Valmiki, his work is not a mere translation or even an adaptation of the Sanskrit epic. Kamban imports into his narration the colour and landscape of his own time. A contemporary of Kamban was the famous poet Auvaiyar who found great happiness in writing for young children. Her works, *Athichoodi* and *Konraiventhan* are even now generally read and taught in schools in Tamil Nadu. Her two other works, *Mooturai* and *Nalvali* were written for slightly older children. All the four works are didactic in character. They explain the basic wisdom that should govern mundane life.

Of the books on the Buddhist and the Jain faiths, the most noteworthy is the *Jivaka-chintamani* by the Jain ascetic Thirutakkadevar composed in the 10th century. *Viruttam* style of poetry was used for the first time for the verses in this book. The five Tamil epics *Jivaka-chintamani*, *Cilappatikaram*, *Manimekalai*, *Kundalakesi* and *Valayapathi* are collectively known as The Five Great Epics of Tamil Literature. There were a number of books written on Tamil grammar. *Yapperungalam* and *Yapperungalakkarigai* were two works on prosody by the Jain ascetic Amirtasagara. Buddamitra wrote *Virasoliyam*, another work on Tamil grammar, during the reign of Virarajendra Chola. *Virasoliyam* attempts to find synthesis between Sanskrit and Tamil grammar. Other grammatical works of this period are *Nannul* by Pavanandi, *Vaccanandi Malai* by Neminatha, and the annotations on the puram theme, *Purapporul Venpamalai* by Aiyanaridanar.

There were biographical and political works such as Jayamkondar's Kalingattuparani, a semi-historical account on the two invasion of Kalinga by Kulothunga Chola I. Jayamkondar was a poet-laureate in the Chola court and his work is a fine example of the balance between fact and fiction the poets had to tread. Ottakuttan, a close contemporary of Kambar, wrote three *Ulas* on Vikrama Chola, Kulothunga Chola II and Rajaraja Chola II

Tamil Muslim literature is eight centuries old. The earliest literary works of this coterie could be traced to the 14th century in the form of *Palsanthmalai*, a small work of eight stanzas. In 1572, Seyku Issaku, better known as Vanna Parimala Pulavar, published *Aayira Masala Venru Vazhankum Adisaya Puranam* detailing the Islamic principles and beliefs in a FAQ format. In 1592, Aali Pulavar wrote the *Mikurasu Malai.*

Vijayanagar and Nayak period

The period from 1300 CE to 1650 was a period of constant change in the political situation of Tamil Nadu. The Tamil country was invaded by the armies of the Delhi Sultanate and defeated the Pandya kingdom. The collapse of the Delhi Sultanate triggered the rise of the Bahmani Sultans in the Deccan. Vijayanagar empire rose from the ashes of the kingdoms of Hoysalas and Chalukyas and eventually conquered the entire south India. The Vijayanagar kings appointed regional governors to rule various territories of their kingdom and Tamil Nadu was ruled by the Madurai Nayaks, Thanjavur Nayaks and

Gingee Nayaks. This period saw a large output of philosophical works, commentaries, epics and devotional poems. A number of monasteries (*Mathas*) were established by the various Hindu sects and these began to play a prominent role in educating the people. Numerous authors were of either the Saiva or the Vaishnava sects. The Vijayanagar kings and their Nayak governors were ardent Hindus and they patronised these *mathas*. Although the kings and the governors of the Vijayanagar empire spoke Kannada and Telugu they encouraged the growth of Tamil literature as we find no slowing down in the literary output during this period.

There was a large output of works of philosophical and religious in nature, such as the *Sivananabodam* by Meykandar. At the end of the 14th century Svarupananda Desikar wrote two anthologies on the philosophy os *Advaita*, the *Sivaprakasapperundirattu*. Arunagirinathar who lived in Tiruvannamalai in the 14th century wrote *Tiruppugal*. Around 1360 verses of unique lilt and set to unique metres these poems are on the god Muruga. Madai Tiruvengadunathar, an official in the court of the Madurai Nayak, wrote *Meynanavilakkam* on the Advaita Vedanta. Siva prakasar, in the early 17th century wrote a number of works on the Saiva philosophy. Notable among these is the *Nanneri* which deals with moral instructions. A considerable par to the religious and philosophical literature of the age took the form of *Puranas* or narrative epics. A number of these were written on the various deities of the temples in Tamil Nadu and are known as Sthala Puranas, based on legend and folklore. One of the most important of the epics was the Mahabharatam by Villiputturar. He translated Vyasa's epic into Tamil and named it *Villibharatam*. *Kanthapuranam* on the god Murugan was written by Kacchiappa Sivachariyar who lived in the 15th century. This work was based broadly on the Sanskrit *Skandapurana*. Varatungarama Pandya, a Pandya king of the period was a littérateur of merit and wrote *Paditrruppattanthathi*. He also translated into Tamil the erotic book known as *Kokkoha* from Sanskrit.

This period also an age of many commentaries of ancient Tamil works. Adiyarkunallar wrote an annotation on Cilappatikaram. Senavaraiyar wrote a commentary on the Tolkappiyam. Then came the famous Parimelalagar whose commentary on the Tirukkural is still considered one of the best available. Other famous annotators such as Perasiriyar and Naccinarikiniyar wrote commentaries on the various work of Sangam literature. The first Tamil dictionary was attempted by Mandalapurusha who compiled the lexicon *Nigandu Cudamani*. Thayumanavar, who lived in the early 18th century, is famous for a number of short poems of philosophical nature.

The 17th century altruist Syed Khader, known colloquially as Seethakaathi, was a great patron of all Tamil poets. He commissioned Umaruppulavar to pen the first biography of Nabi. The collection of poems was called *Seerapuranam*. The 17th century also saw for the first time literary works by Christian authors. Costanzo Giuseppe Beschi (1680–1746), better known as Veeramamunivar, compiled the first dictionary in Tamil. His *Chathurakarathi* was the first to list the Tamil words in alphabetical order. Veeramamunivar is also remembered for his Christian theological epic *Thembavani* on the life and teaching of Jesus Christ.

Modern era

During the 18th and the 19th century Tamil Nadu witnessed some of the most profound changes in the political scene. The traditional Tamil ruling clans were superseded by European colonists and their sympathisers. The Tamil society underwent a deep cultural shock with the imposition of western cultural influences. The Hindu religious establishments attempted to stem the tide of change and to safeguard the Tamil cultural values. Notable among these were the Saiva monasteries at Tiruvavaduthurai, Dharmapuram, Thiruppananthal and Kundrakudi. Meenakshi Sundaram Pillai(1815–1876) was a Tamil scholar who taught Tamil at one of these monasteries. He wrote more than eighty books consisting of over 200,000 poems. He is more famous however for encouraging

U.V.Swaminatha Iyer to go search for Tamil books that have been lost for centuries. Gopalakrishna Bharathi lived during the early 19th century. He wrote numerous poems and lyrics set to tune in Carnatic music. His most famous work is the *Nandan Charitam* on the life of Nandanar who having been born in a sociologically lower caste, faces and overcomes the social obstacles in achieving his dream of visiting the Chidambaram temple. This work is a revolutionary social commentary considering the period in which it was written, although Gopalakrishna Bharati expanded on the story in *Periyapuranam*. Ramalinga Adigal (Vallalar) (1823–1874) wrote the devotional poem *Tiruvarutpa* is considered to be a work of great beauty and simplicity. Maraimalai Adigal (1876–1950) advocated for the purity of Tamil and wanted to clean it of words with Sanskrit influences. One of the great Tamil poets of this period was Subramanya Bharathi. His works are stimulating in their progressive themes like freedom and feminism. Bharathy introduced a new poetic style into the somewhat rigid style of Tamil poetry writing, which had followed the rules set down in the *Tolkaappiyam*. His *puthukkavithai* (Lit.:new poetry) broke the rules and gave poets the freedom to express themselves. He also wrote Tamil prose in the form of commentaries, editorials, short stories and novels. Some of these were published in the Tamil daily *Swadesamitran* and in his Tamil weekly *India*. Inspired by Bharathi, many poets resorted to poetry as a means of reform. Bharathidasan was one such poet. U.V.Swaminatha Iyer, was instrumental in the revival of interest in the Sangam age literature in Tamil Nadu. He travelled all over the Tamil country, collecting, deciphering and publishing ancient books such as *Cilappatikaram*, *Kuruntokai*, etc. He published over 90 books and wrote *En caritham*, an autobiography.

Tamil novel

The novel as a genre of literature arrived in Tamil in the third quarter of the 19th century, more than a century after it became popular with English writers. Its emergence was perhaps facilitated by the growing population of Tamils with a western education and exposure to popular English fiction. Mayavaram Vedanayagam Pillai wrote the first Tamil novel *Prathapa Mudaliar Charithram* in 1879. This was a romance with an assortment of fables, folk tales and even Greek and Roman stories, written with the entertainment of the reader as the principal motive. It was followed by *Kamalambal Charitram* by B. R. Rajam Iyer in 1893 and *Padmavathi Charitram* by A. Madhaviah in 1898. These two portray the life of Brahmins in 19th century rural Tamil Nadu, capturing their customs and habits, beliefs and rituals. Although it was primarily a powerful narration of the common man's life in a realistic style spiced with natural humour, Rajam Iyer's novel has a spiritual and philosophical undertone. Madhaviah tells the story in a more realistic way with a searching criticism of the upper caste society, particularly the sexual exploitation of girls by older men. D.Jayakanthan has enriched the high traditions of literary traditions of Tamil language and contributed towards the shaping of Indian literature. His literature presents a deep and sensitive understanding of complex human nature and is an authentic and vivid index of Indian reality. One famous novel of his is Sila Nerangalil Sila Manithargal. Since the 1990s the post modernist writers emerged as a major figures, including Jeyamohan, S.Ramakrishnan, Charu Nivedita. The critically acclaimed works include Vishnupuram by Jeymohan, Ubapandavam by S.Ramakrishnan, Zero degree by Charu Niveditha, Konangi (Paazhi), yumaa vasuki – Ratha vurvu (Blood Relation), Lakshmi Manivannan (appavin Thottathil neer payum idangal ellam ...), nakulan – ninivu-p-padhai., and Konangi, who mixes classical Tamil inflections with experimental sound poets.

There are other less appreciated works involving those translated from other languages, which are often unrecognized by Tamil pundits. The works include "Urumaatram" (translation of Franz Kafka's *The Metamorphosis*), *Siluvayil Thongum Saathaan* (translation of "Devil on the Cross" by Ngi□g)□wa Thiong'o), *Thoongum azhagigalin Illam* (translation of "House of Sleeping Beauties" by Yasunari Kawabata). Writers like Amarantha, Latha Ramakrishnan are responsible for these works.

Periodicals

The increasing demand of the literate public caused a number of journals and periodicals to be published and these in turn provided a platform for authors to publish their work. *Rajavritti Bodhini* and *Dina Varthamani* in 1855 and Salem Pagadala Narasimhalu Naidu's fortnightlies, Salem *Desabhimini* in 1878 and *Coimbatore Kalanidhi* in 1880, were the earliest Tamil journals. In 1882, G. Subramaniya Iyer started the newspaper *Swadesamitran*. It became the first Tamil daily in 1889. This was the start of many journals to follow and many novelists began to serialise their stories in these journal. The humour magazine *Ananda Vikatan* started by S.S. Vasan in 1929 was to help create some of the greatest Tamil novelists. Kalki Krishnamurthy (1899–1954) serialised his short stories and novels in *Ananda Vikatan* and eventually started his own weekly *Kalki* for which he wrote the enduringly popular novels *Parthiban Kanavu*, *Sivagamiyin Sabadham* and *Ponniyin Selvan*. Pudhumaipithan (1906–1948) was a great writer of short stories and provided the inspiration for a number of authors who followed him. The 'new poetry or *pudukkavithai* pioneered by Bharathi in his prose-poetry was further developed by the literary periodicals *manikkodi* and *ezhuttu* (edited by Si Su Chellappa). Poets such as Mu Metha contributed to these periodicals. Tamil Muslim poets like Kavikko Abdul Rahman, Pavalar Inqulab, Manushyaputhiran and Rajathi Salma too have made significant contributions to social reforms. The pioneering fortnightly journal *Samarasam* was established in 1981 to highlight and cater to the ethnic Tamil Muslim community's issues. Another remarkable work was done in Tamil novel field by Mu.Varatharasanar.[Agal vilakku] [Karithundu]. And last but not least Akilan the unique Tamil novelist, short story writer and a social activist is famous for his works like 'Chithirapavai' 'Vengayinmaindan' 'Pavaivilaku'.

Tamil journalism

The first Tamil periodical was published by the Christian Religious Tract Society in 1831 – *The Tamil Magazine.*

The increasing demand of the literate public caused a number of journals and periodicals to be published and these in turn provided a platform for authors to publish their work. Rajavritti Bodhini and Dina Varthamani in 1855 and Salem Pagadala Narasimhalu Naidu's fortnightlies, Salem Desabhimini in 1878 and Coimbatore Kalanidhi in 1880, were the earliest Tamil journals.

The first regular newspaper in Tamil was Swadesamitran in 1882, started by G.Subramaniya Iyer, editor and sponsor of The Hindu and founding member of the Indian National Congress. He created a whole new Tamil political vocabulary. He) was conscious that those with a knowledge of English are a small number and those with a knowledge of Indian languages the vast majority.

He felt that unless our people were told about the objectives of British rule and its merits and defects in the Indian languages, our political knowledge would never develop. When Subramania Aiyer quit The Hindu 1898, he made the Swadesamitran his full-time business. In 1899, the first Tamil daily. It was to enjoy this status for 17 years.

Subramania Aiyer's "pugnacious style, never qualifying words to soften the sharp tenor of a sentence," his use of words "dipped in a paste of extra pungent green chillies," made the Swadesamitran sought by Tamils wherever they lived in the world. And the daily became even more popular when Subramania Bharati joined it in 1904. The next year, when Lala Lajpat Rai was arrested and agitation followed in the Punjab, Subramania Aiyer's attitude to the British changed and he became a trenchant political critic of the Raj. His whole political mantra can be summed up in these words: `Peaceful but tireless and unceasing effort.' Let us sweat ourselves into Swaraj, he would seem to say." Swadesamitran is credited for coining new Tamil words to deal with science, politics and administration. It had the most comprehensive budget of news among all the regional language papers of that time.

In 1917, *Desabhaktan*, another Tamil daily began with T.V. Kalyansundara Menon as editor. He was succeeded by V.V.S. Iyer, a colleague of the Savarkar brothers. These two editors were scholars with a natural, highly readable but polished style of writing.

The freedom movement and the advent of Gandhi also impacted Tamil journalism. Navasakthi, a Tamil periodical edited by Tamil scholar and freedom fighter V. Kalyanasundaram. C.Rajagopalachari began Vimochanam, a Tamil journal devoted to propagating prohibition at the Gandhi Ashram in Tiruchengode in Salem district.

In 1926, P. Varadarajulu Naidu, who was conducting a Tamil news-cum-views weekly 'Tamil Nadu' started a daily with the same name. Its forceful and colloquial style gained it a wide readership but after the paper failed to take sides with the 1930 Civil Disobedience Movement, the Congress Party decided to bring out a new Tamil daily – India, edited by renowned poet Subramania Bharati. India showed great promise but could not establish itself financially, and folded up soon after Bharati was exiled to Pondicherry. All these papers were published from Madras.

In 1933, the first Tamil tabloid – the 8 page Jayabharati began at a price of D_4 anna. It closed in 1940 as the price could not sustain even its postage.

In September 1934, S. Sadanand (who was running The Free Press Journal) started the Tamil daily Dinamani with T.S. Chockalingam as editor. It was priced at 6 pies, contained bright features and was fearlessly critical. It was highly successful and its circulation eclipsed the total circulation of all other Tamil dailies. Soon 'India' was incorporated into Dinamani. Dinamani made a studied and conscious effort to make the contents of a newspaper intelligible even to the newly literate. In 1935, Viduthalai was begun, but it was more of a views-paper than a newspaper. The Non-Brahman Movement also gave an impetus to Tamil journalism. Newspapers like the *Bharat Devi* were strong supporters of this movement.

Many magazines began in Tamil Nadu during the 1920s and '30s. The humour magazine Ananda Vikatan started by S.S. Vasan in 1929 was to help create some of the greatest Tamil novelists. It is still running successfully after 80 years and the Vikatan group today also publishes Chutti Vikatan, Junior Vikatan, Motor Vikatan and other special interest magazines. R. Krishnamurthy serialised his short stories and novels in Ananda Vikatan and eventually started his own weekly Kalki. The name Kalki denotes the impending tenth Avatar of Lord Vishnu in the Hindu religion, who it is said, will bring to an end the Kali Yuga and reinstate Dharma or righteousness among the worldly beings. He used the name because he wanted to bring about liberation of India.

In 1942, Dina Thanthi (*Daily Telegraph*) was started in Madurai with simultaneous editions in Madras, Salem and Tiruchirappalli. It was founded by S.P. Adithanar, a lawyer trained in Britain. He modeled Thanthi on the style of an English tabloid- The Daily Mirror. He aimed to bring out a newspaper that ordinary people would read, and which would encourage a reading habit even among the newly literate. In the past, the daily newspaper which was printed in Madras reached the southern Tamil region after at least one day. Thanthi used the public bus system to distribute the paper throughout the south Tamil region and capitalized on the hunger for war news that arose after Singapore fell to the Japanese. Due to financial constraints, its Salem and Tiruchirappalli editions had to be closed down for a while. Thanthi emphasized local news, especially crime and the courts. It used photographs extensively and brought banner headlines to Tamil journalism. It could fit one story on an entire broadsheet page, mainly filled with large easy-to-read headlines. One of its biggest scoops was the murder of the editor of a scandalous film magazine by two actors. Thanthi covered the trial in Madras in detail, and its reporters phoned the daily account to the printing centre in Madurai. Thanthi was the first Tamil paper to understand the people's fascination with crime and film stars. The paper was popular and it was said that Tamils learned to read in order to read the newspaper.

Dina Thanthi became one of the largest Tamil language dailies by circulation within a few years; it has been a leading Tamil daily since the 1960s. It has today 14 editions. It is the highest circulated Tamil daily in Bangalore and Pondicherry. It issues a book called 10th, +2 Vina Vidai Book, on every Wednesday during the second part of the year. The model question papers of all the subjects of Standard 10 and 12 are provided with answers along with the question papers of board exams that are conducted previous year.

Popular fiction

Crime and detective fiction has enjoyed wide popularity in Tamil Nadu since the 1930s. Popular authors in the years before independence included Kurumbur Kuppusami and Vaduvur Duraisami Iyengar. In the 1950s and '60s, Tamilvanan's detective hero Shankarlal carried readers to a variety of foreign locales, while using a pure Tamil with very few Hindi or English loan words. These writers are often extremely prolific, with hundreds or even thousands of short novels to their credit, and one or more short novel published in a monthly periodical. Indra Soundar Rajan, another popular modern author, writes supernatural crime thrillers usually based around Hindu mythology.

In the 1940s and 1950s Kalki Krishnamurthy was notable for his historical and social fiction.

In the 1950s and 60s, Chandilyan wrote a number of very popular historical romance novels set in medieval India or on medieval trade routes with Malaysia, Indonesia and Europe.

From the 1950s, spanning six decades, Jayakanthan authored around 40 novels, 200 short stories, apart from two autobiographies. Outside literature, he made two films. In addition, four of his other novels were adapted into films by others. His works revolve around the lives of underclass people like rickshaw-pullers, prostitutes and rag-pickers.

Arunaa Nandhini is one of recent Tamil novelists who has entered the hearts of many Tamil readers, and her story covers family subject, romance, reality, with some humor added for the readers to enjoy their leisure.

Modern romance novels are represented by the current bestselling author in the Tamil language, Ramanichandran.

Though sales of Tamil pulp fiction have declined since the hey-day of the mid-1990s, and many writers have turned to the more lucrative television serial market, there remains a thriving scene.

New media

The rise of the Internet has triggered a dramatic growth in the number of Tamil blogs and specialist portals catering to political and social issues. Tamil literature is even available in the form of e-books.

5

Geography and Flora & Fauna

WILDLIFE OF TAMIL NADU

There are more than 2000 species of fauna that can be found in Tamil Nadu. This rich wildlife is attributed to the diverse relief features as well as favorable climate and vegetation in the Indian state. Recognizing the state's role in preserving the current environment, the government has established several wildlife and bird sanctuaries as well as national parks, which entail stringent protective measures. Tamil Nadu is also included in the International Network of Biosphere Reserves, which facilitates international recognition and additional funding. Currently, there are five national parks and 17 sanctuaries that serve as homes to the wildlife.

Mammals

Tamil Nadu is known for the diversity of its mammals due to the varying environs that sustain both dry and moist deciduous forests. Notable species include Arboreal animals distributed in its hills, grasslands, mangroves, scrubs and forests. These also include rare and vulnerable species like the Bengal tiger, Nilgiri Tahr, and the lion-tailed macaque. The other mammals found in Tamil Nadu include:

Asian elephant, Indian leopard, sloth bear, gaur, Manjampatti white bison, wild boar, lion-tailed macaque, Nilgiri langur, common langur, bonnet macaque, four-horned antelope, dhole, tree shrew, sambar deer, mouse deer, muntjac, jungle cat, fishing cat, leopard cat, small Indian civet, toddy cat, Asian small mongoose, blackbuck, chital, striped hyena, Nilgiri marten, Travancore flying squirrel, grizzled giant squirrel, flying squirrel, three-striped palm squirrel, black-naped hare, grey slender loris, Indian pangolin, Asian small-clawed otter and Malabar spiny dormouse, Indian fox, bare-bellied hedgehog, Indian porcupine, smooth-coated otter.

Endangered Nilgiri tahr, state animal of Tamil Nadu

Birds

These include the Malabar trogon, Malabar pied hornbill, Nilgiri wood-pigeon, Nilgiri laughing thrush, peregrine falcon, Bonelli's eagle, dollarbird, Nilgiri pipit, little spiderhunter, white-bellied shortwing, little ringed plover, Indian swiftlet, white-bellied treepie, white-bellied woodpecker, green imperial pigeon, Nilgiri flycatcher, great eared nightjar, grey junglefowl, heart-spotted woodpecker, peafowl, grey-fronted green pigeon, wood sandpiper, vernal hanging parrot, Malabar parakeet, white-browed bulbul, stork-billed kingfisher, grey-headed fish-eagle, brown-capped pygmy woodpecker, black-and-orange flycatcher, brown-headed barbet, blue-bearded bee-eater, broad-tailed grassbird, cormorant, darter, heron, egret, open-billed stork, spoonbilland white ibis, little grebe, Indian moorhen, black-winged stilt, a few migratory ducks and occasionally a grey pelican.

Marine species

These include the dugong, turtle, dolphin and *Balanoglossus*.

Insects

Butterflies: southern birdwing, common rose, crimson rose, common bluebottle, common jay, tailed jay, spot swordtail, five-bar swordtail, common mime, lime, Malabar banded swallowtail, Malabar raven, red Helen, common Mormon, blue Mormon, paris peacock, Malabar banded peacock, common banded peacock, common emigrant, mottled emigrant, small grass yellow, common grass yellow, common Jezebel, Psyche, common gull, lesser gull, pioneer or caper white, plain puffin, chocolate albatross, common albatross, lesser albatross, small orange tip, white orange tip, yellow orange tip, common wanderer, great orange tip

Reptiles

Mugger crocodile, king cobra, bamboo pit viper, Indian python, Travancore tortoise, spectacled cobra, common krait, common green whip snake, Russell's kukri, common Indian monitor, Indian chameleon, Oriental garden lizard, South Indian flying lizard, olive ridley turtle, Cochin forest cane turtle, Indian black turtle, Russell's viper, various species of skinks and geckos.

FLORA AND FAUNA

Tamil Nadu is rich in flora and fauna and some of its major wildlife sanctuaries like Mudumalai and Annamalai (or Indira Gandhi Wildlife Sanctuary), are situated in the Western Ghats.

These hills are ideal havens for elephants, tigers, bison, monkeys and deer. Of the 3,000 and more plant species found in Tamil Nadu, a majority is found in the mixed deciduous forests of this region.

One of the most noteworthy flowers is the Kurinji of Kodaikanal, which blooms once in 12 years. Cinchona, from which the anti-malarial drug quinine is extracted, and the medicinal eucalyptus grow, abundantly in the Nilgiri hills. Forests of other medicinal herbs are found in Palani hills and Courtallam.

Palmyra trees grow profusely in Tirunelveli and its products are used as raw materials for several cottage industries. Rubber is the main plantation crop in Kanyakumari and sandalwood grows in the Javadhu hills of Vellore district.

Flora and Fauna of Tamil Nadu

A wide range of large, naturally occurring community of Flora and Fauna of Tamil Nadu Nadu extending east from the South Western Ghats montane rain backwoods in the Western Ghats through the South Deccan Plateau dry deciduous woods and Deccan thistle bush woodlands to tropical dry broadleaf timberlands and after that to the shorelines, estuaries, salt swamps, mangroves, and coral reefs of the Bay of Bengal. The state has a variety of widely varied vegetation with numerous species and environments. To safeguard this assorted qualities of untamed life there are Protected areas of Tamil Nadu and also biospheres which ensure bigger regions of natural surroundings regularly incorporate at least one or more National Parks.

Nilgiri mountains

At least 24 of the Nilgiri mountains' peaks are above 2,000 metres (6,600 ft), the highest peak being Doddabetta, at 2,637 metres (8,652 ft). The Nilgiri Hills are part of the Nilgiri Biosphere Reserve (itself part of the UNESCO World Network of Biosphere Reserves.), and form a part of the protected bio reserves in India. The highest waterfall, Kolakambai Fall, north of Kolakambai hill, has an unbroken fall of 400 ft (120 m). Nearby is the 150 ft (46 m) Halashana falls. Over 2,700 species of flowering plants, 160 species of fern and fern allies, countless types of flowerless plants, mosses, fungi, algae, and land lichens are found in the sholas of the Nilgiris. No other hill station has so many exotic species.

Indira Gandhi Wildlife Sanctuary and National Park

The park is named after former Prime Minister of India Indira Gandhi who visited the park on 7 October 1961. "Topslip" located in the northeast corner of the park is derived from the local 19th century practice of sliding timber logs down the hills from here. Indira Gandhi Wildlife Sanctuary and National Park (IGWLS&NP) is a protected area.

Threatened species of mammals in the sanctuary include – the endangered Bengal tiger, Indian elephant, dhole (Asiatic wild dog), Nilgiri tahr and lion-tailed macaque, the vulnerable brown mongoose, gaur, Malabar spiny dormouse, Nilgiri langur, rusty-spotted cat, sambar deer, sloth bear and smooth-coated otter, the near threatened Indian giant squirrel, Indian leopard and Indian pangolin. The park is home to a wide variety of flora and fauna of Tamilnadu, typical of the South Western Ghats. There are over 2000 species plants of which about 400 species are of prime medicinal value. The diverse topography and rainfall gradient allow a wide variety of vegetation comprising a mix of natural and man-made habitats.

Mudumalai National Park

The Mudumalai National Park and Wildlife Sanctuary also a declared tiger reserve, lies on the northwestern side of the Nilgiri Hills (Blue Mountains), in Nilgiri District, about 150 kilometres (93 mi) north-west of Coimbatore city in Tamil Nadu. The protected area is home to several endangered and vulnerable species including Indian elephant, Bengal tiger, gaur and Indian leopard. There are at least 266 species of birds in the sanctuary, including critically endangered Indian white-rumped vulture and long-billed vulture. There are 48 tigers in the Nilgiri Reserve across which tigers are free to roam. Moist bamboo brakes are found amidst dry deciduous, moist deciduous and semi-evergreen forests and along the fringes of riparian forests and swamps. This sanctuary is home to several species of wild relatives of cultivated plants including wild rice, wild ginger, turmeric, cinnamon, solanum, guava, mango and pepper that act as a reserve gene pool for the cultivated plants.

Mukurthi National Park

The park is characterised by montane grasslands and shrublands interspersed with sholas in a high altitude area of high rainfall, near-freezing temperatures and high winds. It is home to an array of endangered wildlife, including royal Bengal tiger and Asian elephant, but its main mammal attraction is the Nilgiri tahr. The park was previously known as Nilgiri Tahr National Park. The park is a part of Nilgiri Biosphere Reserve, India's first International Biosphere Reserve. As part of the Western Ghats, it is a UNESCO World Heritage Site since 1 July 2012.

Gulf of Mannar Marine National Park

The Gulf of Mannar Marine National Park is a protected area of India consisting of 21 small islands (islets) and adjacent coral reefs in the Gulf of Mannar in the Indian Ocean. The park includes estuaries, mudflats, beaches and forests of the near shore environment. It also includes marine components such as coral reefs, seaweed communities, sea grasses, salt marshes and mangroves. Seaweed photo gallery.

Guindy National Park

Guindy National Park is, located in Chennai, South India, is the 8th smallest National Park of India and one of the very few national parks situated inside a city. The park has a role in both ex-situ and in-situ conservation and is home to 400 blackbucks, 2,000 spotted deers, 24 jackals, a wide variety of snakes, geckos, tortoises and over 130 species of birds, 14 species of mammals, over 60 species of butterflies and spiders each, a wealth of different invertebrates—grasshoppers, ants, termites, crabs, snails, slugs, scorpions, mites, earthworms, millipedes, and the like. These are free-ranging fauna and live with the minimal of interference from human beings. The only major management activity is protection as in any other in-situ conservation area. The park attracts more than 700,000 visitors every year.

6

Economy

ECONOMY OF TAMIL NADU

Tamil Nadu has the second-largest economy in India. Over 50% of the state is urbanized, accounting for 9.6% of the urban population in the country, while only comprising 6% of India's total population. Services contributes to 45% of the economic activity in the state, followed by manufacturing at 34% and agriculture at 21%. Government is the major investor in the state, with 52% of total investments, followed by private Indian investors at 29.9% and foreign private investors at 14.9%. It has been ranked as the second most economically free state in India by the Economic Freedom Rankings for the States of India.

Macroeconomic trend

This is a chart of trend of gross state domestic product of Tamil Nadu at market prices estimated in Crore Indian rupees.

Year	Gross state domestic product
2011	751,910 crore (US$100 billion)
2015	976,703 crore (US$140 billion)
2017	1,596,810 crore (US$220 billion)
2019	2,183,000 crore (US$300 billion)(RE)

AGRICULTURE AND LIVESTOCK

Tamil Nadu has historically been an agricultural state, while its advances in other fields transformed the state into being an industrialized and innovation based economy, leading to competition for land and its resources. Agriculture is heavily dependent on the river water and monsoon rains. The perennial rivers are Palar, Cheyyar, Ponnaiyar, Kaveri, Meyar, Bhavani, Amaravathi, Vaigai, Chittar and Tamaraparani. Non-perennial rivers include the Vellar, Noyyal, Suruli, Siruvani, Gundar, Vaipar, Valparai and Varshali. Tamil Nadu is the highest producer of bananas and coconuts in the whole country. It is also a leading state in production of other crops such as sugarcane, cotton, kambu, corn, rye, groundnut and oil seeds. At present, Tamil Nadu is India's 4th largest producer of rice behind West Bengal, Uttar Pradesh and Punjab Tamil Nadu is the home to Dr. M. S. Swaminathan, known as the "father of the Green Revolution" in India. The state is one of the major producers of turmeric in India.

Given below is a table of 2015-16 national output share of select agricultural crops and allied segments in Tamil Nadu based on 2011 prices

Segment	National Share %
Drumstick	98.0
Tapioca	44.4
Floriculture	16.5
Gooseberry	18
Coconut	29.1
Tamarind	25.3
Meat	7.5
Turmeric	14.6
Banana	19.4
Ragi	17.8
Horsegram	17.5
Sapota	17.4

Urd	14.7
Groundnut	14.2
Cucumber	12.6
Maize	12.3
Egg	12.2
Carrot	12.1
Marine fish	11.8
Gur	11.6
Water melon	11.4
Jackfruit	10.9
Jowar	10.6
Tea	8.5
Cocoa	8.2
Moong	7.9
Oilseed	7.7
Papaya	7.4
Paddy	6.9
Bean	6.7
Fruit and vegetable	6.3
Sugarcane	6.1
Mango	5.8
Bitter gourd	5.6
Pear	5.3
Sericulture and Apiculture	5.3

INDUSTRY AND MANUFACTURING

One of the global electrical equipment public sector company BHEL has manufacturing plants at Tiruchirappalli and Ranipet. The Tamil Nadu state government owns the Tamil Nadu Newsprint and Papers (TNPL), the world's biggest bagasse-based paper mills in Karur as well as the world's sixth largest manufacturer of watches together with TATA, under the brand name of "Titan" which has manufacturing plant in Coimbatore. 40 percent of all wind-generated electricity in India is created by windmills in Tamil Nadu. Danish wind power company

NEG Micon has established its manufacturing unit in Chennai. Tamil Nadu is a leading producer of cement in India and with manufacturing units located at Ariyalur, Coimbatore and Tirunelveli.

High-density PolyEthylene (HDPE) mono filament yarn and associated products are manufactured in Karur for mosquito nets and fishing nets. More than 60% mosquito nets in India are manufactured here. The region around Salem is rich in mineral ores. The country's largest steel public sector undertaking, SAIL, has a steel plant in Salem.

Coimbatore is major Industrial hub in South India and it houses more than 30,000 small, medium and large industries. Coimbatore is known as "Manchester of South India" due to its extensive textile industry and also referred to as "the Pump City" as it supplies half or 50% of India's requirements of motors and pumps. The city is one of the largest exporters of textile, jewellery, wet grinders, poultry and auto components and the term "Coimbatore Wet Grinder" has been given a Geographical indication. Larsen & Toubro has 300 acre huge manufacturing campus in Coimbatore which houses various units of company, manufactures aerospace and defence parts for leading players in the market.

Thoothukudi is known as "Gateway of Tamilnadu". Thoothukudi is the major chemical producer in the state. It produces the 70 percent of the total salt production in the state and 30 percent in the country.

Automotive

Chennai is nicknamed as "The Detroit of Asia". Chennai is home to large number of auto component industries. Over 11.2% of the *S&P CNX 500* conglomerates have corporate offices in Tamil Nadu. Tamil Nadu has manufacturing facilities from automobiles, railway coaches, battle-tanks, tractors, motorbikes and heavy vehicles to ships.

Alstom has a manufacturing facility in Coimbatore which manufactures rail transportation products.

Vehicle Parts Manufacturers

MRF the local tyre manufacturer is located in Chennai and Perambalur. TI cycles of Murugappa group have their units in Chennai. UCAL Carburettors, TRW Rane, TVS Group are established in Hosur.TVS Srichakra Tyre works at Madurai. Coimbatore is home to Pricol, Elgi Equipments, Craftsman, Roots Horn, Rolon Chains and numerous Tier-I part suppliers.

Transportation Industry

About 40 per cent of the trucks operated in the State are from Tiruchengode, Sankagiri, Namakkal and an area noted for its truck body building; over 18,000 trucks. Karur is well known for its bus body building industries where most of the coaches for buses used in south India are built. Heavy load trucks 12 and 14 wheels trucks are operated mostly from Sankagiri region. Tiruchengode is famous for borewell drilling industry.

Textiles

Tamil Nadu is the largest textile hub of India. Coimbatore often referred as the "Manchester of South India" due to its cotton production and textile industries. The textile industry plays a significant role in the Indian economy by providing direct employment to an estimated 35 million people, and thereby contributing 4% of GDP and 35% of gross export earnings. The textile sector contributes to 14% of the manufacturing sector. From Spinning to garment manufacturing, entire textile production chain facilities are in Tamil Nadu. About half of India's total spinning mill capacity is in Tamil Nadu. The western part of Tamil Nadu comprising Coimbatore, Tirupur, Erode , Karur and Dindigul has the majority of spinning mills manufacturing cotton/polyester/ blended yarn, open end yarn and silk yarn used by garment units in Tamil Nadu, Maharastra etc. Yarn is also exported to China, Bangladesh etc. Tirupur knitted garment units have been exporting garments for about 3 decades with 2015-16 exports in the range of USD 3 Billion. Karur is the major home textile (Curtain cloth, bed linens, kitchen linens, toilet linens, table linens, wall hangings etc.) manufacturing and export hub in India. Erode is the main cloth market in south India for both retail and wholesale ready-mades. Madras (Chennai) has a large presence of woven garments (shirts/pants) manufacturing units. Madurai and Kanchipuram are famous for handloom sarees exported / sold all over India. Lakshmi Machine Works [LMW], one of the three major textile machinery manufacturing companies in the world is located in Coimbatore. Savio also has a factory in Coimbatore. Many textile component manufacturers are in Coimbatore and some export to the Europe etc.

Aeroscape and Defence

The defence industry in Tamil Nadu is one of the fastest growing sector in the states generating a huge amount of export revenue. The states serves as the headquarters for numerous defence manufacturing public undertakings such as Heavy Vehicles Factory, Combat Vehicles Research and Development Establishment, Ordnance Factory Tiruchirappalli, L&T Aerospace & Defence unit Coimbatore, LMW Advanced Technology Centre, Coimbatore, Ashok Leyland Defence Systems, Mahindra Aerospace, Ramco Systems, TANEJA Aerospace and Salem Aerospace Limited. The state has the country's first defence corridor and aerospace park. The principal cities manufacturing defence and aerospace components are Chennai, Coimbatore, Tiruchirappalli, Salem and the secondary manufacturing cities are Nagercoil, Hosur,. French aerospace and defence company, Airbus decided to invest 1 billion dollar (7,200 crores) in a aerospace project in Chennai. The company has also planned to built an helicopter assembly factory in Tamil Nadu. Tier - II cities of Coimbatore and Salem also serves as a major export hub for defence manufacturing firms. Defence, paramilitary and police personnel across the nation use guns, ammunitions and bullets manufactured from the city. Special grade steel used in making missiles are manufactured in Salem. India's multinational engineering conglomerate L&T joint venture with france based MBDA, a world leader in missile systems planned a "L&T MBDA Missile Systems" facility at Aspen SEZ in Coimbatore serves as its hub to export fully assembled missile systems to Europe.

Tejas Flight

Tamil Nadu also is the hub station where the first Indian made Fifth-generation jet fighter plane is to be manufactured. The Aeronautical Development Agency, which conceived and designed the Light Combat Aircraft (LCA) Tejas, set the ball rolling for building the next generation defence aircraft, the Advanced Medium Combat Aircraft (AMCA), by initiating in Coimbatore to build a technology demonstrator. The project — to be implemented in Sulur in Coimbatore district which will house the permanent base of the Tejas squadron — marks one of Tamil Nadu's first major defence aircraft project.

Electronics

Electronics manufacturing is a growing industry in Tamil Nadu. Chennai has emerged as EMS Hub of India. Companies like Flextronics, Motorola, Sony-Ericsson, Foxconn, Samsung, Cisco, and Dell have chosen Chennai as their South Asian manufacturing hub. Products manufactured include circuit boards and cellular phone handsets. Ericsson also has a Research and Development facility in Chennai. Big EPC companies have set up their Engineering centres which include Saipem India Projects Ltd, Technip, Foster Wheeler, Schneider Electric, Mott MacDonald, Petrofac, Austrian company "Austrian Energy and Environment" have also a design office here besides local giant ECC Larsen & Toubro. Sanmina-SCI is the latest company to invest in Tamil Nadu to create a state of the art manufacturing facility. Nokia Siemens Networks has decided to build a manufacturing plant for wireless network equipment in Tamil Nadu.

The state with a projected population of about 66.5 million in year 2009 has a high mobile market share in India. According to statistics released by Telecom Regulatory Authority of India (TRAI), the state had a total subscriber base of 43 million mobile customers at the beginning of August 2009.

Leather

Tamil Nadu accounts for 60 per cent of leather tanning capacity in India and 38 per cent of all leather footwear, garments and components. The state also accounts for 50 per cent of leather exports from India, valued at around US$3.3 billions of the total US$6.5 billion from India. Hundreds of leather and tannery facilities are located around Vellore and its nearby towns, such as Ranipet, Ambur and Vaniyambadi. The Vellore district is the top exporter of finished leather goods in the country. Vellore leather accounts for more than 37 percent of the country's export of leather and leather-related products (such as finished leathers, shoes, garments and gloves).

Hundreds of leather and tannery industries are located around Vellore, Dindigul and Erode its nearby towns such as Ranipet, Ambur, Perundurai and Vaniyambadi. The tanning industry in India has a total capacity of 225 million pieces of hides and skins, of which Tamil Nadu alone contributes 70 per cent, a leading export product share at 40 per cent for India. It currently employs about 2.5 million persons. Leather exports by the end of 2000–2001 were INR90 billion.

Central Leather Research Institute (CLRI), a CSIR research laboratory, is located in Chennai, the state capital.

Fireworks

The town of Sivakasi is a leader in the areas of printing, fireworks, and safety matches. It was fondly called as "Little Japan" by Jawaharlal Nehru. It contributes to 80% of India's fireworks production. Sivakasi provides over 60% of India's total offset printing solutions.

BANKING

The first modern bank in Tamil Nadu, Bank of Madras was started by the Britishers in 1843. It was followed by the opening of other banks namely - Arbuthnot & Co, Bank of Chettinad, Bank of Madura, that were latter merged under the supervision of RBI. The state serves as the headquarters for the second most number of banks in India, only next to the financial Capital Mumbai. The banking sector in Tamil Nadu is broadly classified into scheduled banks and non-scheduled banks.All banks included in the Second Schedule to the Reserve Bank of India Act, 1934 are Scheduled Banks. These banks comprise Scheduled Commercial Banks and Scheduled Co-operative Banks. Scheduled Co-operative Banks consist of Scheduled State Co-operative Banks and Scheduled Urban Cooperative Banks. Scheduled Commercial Banks in Tamil Nadu are categorised into five different groups according to their ownership and/or nature of operation:

- Nationalised Banks
- Private Sector Banks
- Foreign Banks
- Regional Rural Banks
- Small Finance Banks

Mining

This is a chart of proven reserves of major minerals of Tamil Nadu in 2001 by *Department of Geology and Mining* with figures in tonnes.

Mineral	Reserve	National Share %
Lignite	30,275,000	87
Vermiculite	2,000,000	66
Garnet	23,000,000	42
Zircon	8,000,000	38
Graphite	2,000,000	33
Ilmenite	98,000,000	28
Rutile	5,000,000	27
Monazite	2,000,000	25
Magnesite	73,000,000	17

Tamil Nadu has a few mining projects based on Titanium, Lignite, Magnesite, Graphite, Limestone, Granite and Bauxite. The first one is the Neyveli Lignite Corporation that has led development of large industrial complex around Neyveli in Cuddalore district with Thermal power plants, Fertilizer, Brequetting and Carbonisation plants. Tata Iron and Steel Company (TISCO) have entered into MoU with Government of Tamil Nadu in June 2002 for establishing a titanium dioxide (TiO2) plant with a project outlay of $650 million. Magnesite mining is done at Salem apart from which mining of Bauxite ores are carried out at Yercaud and this region is also rich in Iron Ore Kanjamalai. Molybdenum is found in Dharmapuri, and is the only source in the country.

ENERGY

Tamil Nadu, being an industrialized and urbanized state, is among the top 3 states with respect to generation of electricity. The total installed capacity of Tamil Nadu stands at around 30200 MW as in September 2018, that derives 11500 MW of power from solar and wind energy. Tamil Nadu has the distinction of being the leader in renewable energy In India by adopting clean sources of energy and having established wind farms as early as 1995. Today it produces more wind power than Denmark and the Netherlands.

Wind Energy

The Tamil Nadu Energy Development Agency (TEDA) is a Tamil Nadu government promoting renewable energy sources and energy conservation activities. The agency has largely been responsible for instigating the tremendous growth of Tamil Nadu in the development of wind power. The total installed capacity of windmills in Tamil Nadu totals to around 8700MW. Muppandal wind farm is a renewable energy source, supplying the villagers with electricity for work. Wind farms were built in Nagercoil and Tuticorin apart from already existing ones around Coimbatore, Pollachi, Dharapuram and Udumalaipettai.

Solar

In March 2008, Signet Solar Inc. signed a memorandum of understanding with the State government to build a INR 20 billion thin-film silicon photovoltaic modulemanufacturing plant in the Sriperumbudur Special Economic Zone. In June 2008, Moser Baer inked a MoU with the state government to build INR 20 billion plant for manufacturing of silicon-based photovoltaic thin film modules and allied products in the Oragadam Special Economic Zone which is closer to the Signet Solar's plant in sriperumbudur.

Nuclear

The Kalpakkam Nuclear Power Plant, Ennore Thermal Plant, Neyveli Lignite Power Plant, Virudhachalam Ceramics and the Narimanam Natural Gas Plants are major sources of Tamil Nadu's electricity. It is presently adding the Koodankulam Nuclear Power Plant to its energy grid. Tamil Nadu sources some of its power needs from renewable sources with wind power contributing over 2000 MW or over 20% of the needs. Tamil Nadu is facing largest power shortage in 2013 (34.1% deficit), the highest in the country, due to industrialization over the last decade. India's leading steel producer SAIL has a steel plant in Salem, Tamil Nadu. Tamil Nadu ranks first nationwide in diesel-based thermal electricity generation with national market share of over 34%.

Hydel

The Mettur Dam is one of the largest dams in India. It was completed in 1936. The total length of the dam is 1700 meters. It is also called Stanley Reservoir. The Mettur Hydro Electrical power project is also quite large Mettur Dam. Mettur has a number of industries (50 km from Salem city): SISCOL, MALCO (Madras Aluminium Company owned by Vedanta Resources), Chemplast (former known as Mettur Chemicals), Thermal power plant, Hydel power plant and huge number of chemical industries. There are many other dams that provide irrigation and drinking water, including the Vaigai Dam.

Bio-diesel

Tamil Nadu at this time is the only state to have a formal Bio-Diesel Policy to use jatropha crops as a source of biofuel and to distribute wasteland to the poor farmers for the planting of these crops.

TRANSPORTATION

Kathipara Junction in Chennai

Tamil Nadu has a well established transportation system that connects all parts of the state. This is partly responsible for the investment in the state. Though the present transportation system is substantial, it needs to be developed further to keep pace with the rapid increase in use. Tamil Nadu is served by an extensive road network in terms of its spread and quality, providing links between urban centres, agricultural market-places and rural habitations in the countryside.

Road

There are 28 national highways in the state, covering a total distance of 5,036 km (3,129 mi). The state is also a terminus for the Golden Quadrilateral project that is 99.2% completed as of 31 July 2010. Chennai CMBT and Erode Central Bus Terminus are the largest and the second largest bus terminals in Tamil Nadu respectively. The state has a total road length of 167,000 km, of which 60,628 km are maintained by Highways Department. This is nearly 2.5 times higher than the density of all-India road network. It ranks second with a share of over 20% in total road projects under operation in the public-private partnership (PPP) model. It is currently working on upgrading its road network, though the pace of work is considered slow.

Rail

Tamil Nadu has a well-developed rail network as part of Southern Railway. Headquartered at Chennai, the present Southern Railway network extends over a large area of India's Southern Peninsula, covering the states of Tamil Nadu, Kerala, Puducherry, minor portions of Karnataka and Andhra Pradesh. Tamil Nadu has a total railway track length of 6,693 km and there are 690 railway stations in the state. The system connects it with most major cities in India. Main rail junctions in the state include Chennai, Coimbatore, Erode, Madurai, Salem, Tiruchirapalli and Tirunelveli . Chennai has a well-established Suburban Railway network, a Mass Rapid Transport System and is currently developing a Metro system, with its first underground stretch operational since May 2017.

Air

Tamil Nadu has a major international airport, Chennai International Airport, that is connected with 19 countries with more than 400 direct flights every day. Other international airports in Tamil Nadu include Coimbatore International Airport, Madurai International Airport and Tiruchirapalli International Airport. Chennai International Airport is currently the third largest airport in India after Mumbai and Delhi and has a passenger growth of 18%. It also has domestic airports at Tuticorin, Salem and Madurai make several parts of the state easily accessible. Increased industrial activity has given rise to an increase in passenger traffic as well as freight movement which has been growing at over 18 per cent per year.

Ports

Tamil Nadu has three major ports at Chennai, Ennore, Kattupalli and Tuticorin, as well as one intermediate port, Nagapattinam, and seven minor ports, Rameswaram, Kanyakumari, Cuddalore, Colachel, Karaikal, Pamban and Valinokkam of which are currently capable of handling over 73 million metric tonnes of cargo annually (24 per cent share of India). All the minor ports are managed by the Tamil Nadu Maritime Board. Chennai Port is an artificial harbour situated on the Coromandel Coast in South-East India and it is the second principal port in the country for handling containers. It is currently being upgraded to have a dedicated terminal for cars capable of handling 400,000 vehicles by 2009 to be used by Hyundai, Ford and Nissan Renault. Ennore Port was recently converted from an intermediate port to a major port and handles all the coal and ore traffic in Tamil Nadu. The volume of cargo in the ports grew by 13 per cent over 2005. The Tuticorin Port is expanding its facilities at the cost of US$1.6 billion. The Sethusamudram Shipping Canal Project will transform the Tuticorin port into a transshipment hub similar to those in Singapore and Colombo. The ports are in need of improvement and some of them have container terminals privatised.

Tourism

The Western Ghats in Kanyakumari District, near the southern end of the range.

Tamil Nadu has since ancient past, has been a hub for tourism. In recent years, the state has emerged as one of the leading tourist destination for both domestic and foreign tourists. Tourism in Tamil Nadu is promoted by Tamil Nadu Tourism Development Corporation (TTDC), a Government of Tamil Nadu undertaking. The state currently ranks the highest among Indian states with about 248 million arrivals in 2013. The annual growth rate of the industry stood at 16 per cent. Approximately 2,804,687 foreign and 111,637,104 domestic tourists visited the state in 2010.

The state boasts some of the grand Hindu temples built in Dravidian architecture. The Brihadishwara Temple in Thanjavur, built by the Cholas, the Airavateswara temple in Darasuram and the Shore Temple, along with the collection of other monuments in Mahabalipuram (also called Mamallapuram) have been declared as UNESCO World Heritage Sites. Madurai is home to the Madurai Meenakshi

Amman Temple. Sri Ranganathaswamy Temple, Srirangam is the largest functioning temple in the world, Tiruchirappalli where the famous Rockfort Temple is located, Rameshwaram whose temple walk-ways corridor (Praagarams) are the longest 1.2 km (0.75 mi) of all Indian temples in the world, Kanchipuram and Palani are important pilgrimage sites for Hindus.

Other popular temples in Tamil Nadu include those in Gangaikonda Cholapuram, Chidambaram, Thiruvannaamalai, Tiruchendur, Tiruvarur, Kumbakonam, Srivilliputhur, Tiruttani, Namakkal, Vellore, Karur, Bhavani, Coimbatore, Kanniyakumari.

Shore Temple, Mahabalipuram(built in 700–728 AD) in Tamil Nadu

Tamil Nadu is also home to hill stations like Udhagamandalam (Ooty), Kodaikanal, Yercaud, Coonoor, Topslip, Valparai, Yelagiri and Manjolai.

The Nilgiri hills, Palani hills, Shevaroy hills, Kolli Hills and Cardamom hills are all abodes of thick forests and wildlife. Tamil Nadu has many National Parks, Biosphere Reserves, Wildlife Sanctuaries, Elephant and Bird Sanctuaries, Reserved

Forests, Zoos and Crocodile farms. Prominent among them are Mudumalai National Park, The Gulf of Mannar Biosphere Reserve, Anaimalai Wildlife Sanctuary, Vedanthangal Bird Sanctuary and Arignar Anna Zoological Park.

The mangrove forests at Pichavaram are also eco-tourism spots of importance.

Kanyakumari, the southernmost tip of peninsular India, is famous for its beautiful sunrise, Vivekananda Rock Memorial and Thiruvalluvar's statue built off the coastline.

Marina Beach in Chennai is one of the longest beaches in the world. The stretch of beaches from Chennai to Mahabalipuram are home to many resorts, theme parks and eateries.

The prominent waterfalls in the state are Courtallam, Hogenakkal, Papanasam, Manimuthar, Thirparappu, Pykara and Silver Cascade. The Chettinad region of the state is renowned for its Palatial houses and cuisine. With medical care in Chennai, Vellore, Coimbatore and Madurai, Tamil Nadu has the largest numbers in Medical tourism in India.

Services

Tamil Nadu has 526 engineering colleges, the most for any state in India giving the services industry access to qualified and skilled labour force. The state has a wide network of about 110 industrial parks and estates offering developed plots with supporting infrastructure. Also, the state government is promoting other industrial parks like Rubber Park, Apparel Parks, Floriculture Park, TIDEL Park for IT/ITS, TICEL BioPark for Biotechnology, Siruseri IT Park, Elcot SEZ and Agro Export Zones among others. Tamil Nadu has the largest number of Small and medium enterprises (SMEs) in India.

Software Parks

This is a chart of trend of software exports from Tamil Nadu published by Electronics Corporation of Tamil Nadu with figures in Crores of Indian Rupees.

Year	Software exports
1995	370 crore (US$51 million)
2000	31,160 crore (US$4.3 billion)
2005	41,150 crore (US$5.7 billion)
2010	62,100 crore (US$8.6 billion)
2013	82,450 crore (US$11 billion)
2017	111,179 crore (US$15 billion)

Chennai is the third largest software exporter in India, next to Bangalore and Hyderabad. India's largest IT park is housed at Chennai.

Software exports from Tamil Nadu during 2017-2018 rose 8.6% per cent to touch 1,11,179 crore, involving a workforce of 780,000. Chennai is the largest hub for e-publishing, as there are 67 e-publishing units registered with the STPI in Chennai and 25 in Bangalore.

Companies such as HCL, Wipro, TCS, L&T, Satyam, Infosys, IBM,Zeesta (Adalricos), Cognizant Technology Solutions, Covansys, Xansa, Verizon, iSoft, Electronic Data Systems, Bally and many others have offices in Chennai.

Infosys Technologies has set up India's largest software development centre to house 25,000 software professionals at an estimated investment of 12,500 million (US$170 million) in Chennai. India's largest IT park – SIPCOT is housed at Siruseri – Chennai, It has numerous IT companies such as TCS, CTS, Syntel, Steria, Polaris, Patni, Hexaware etc.

Chennai has been rated as the most attractive city for offshoring services. Coimbatore is second largest Software exporter in Tamil Nadu with presence of Amazon, Bosch, Cognizant, Ford, NTT Data, TCS, Wipro, HCL, Altran, Harman, Deloitte. Cognizant has more than 13,000 employees working in Coimbatore, which is their second largest headcount in India after Chennai. Bosch has one of the largest R&D development centre in Coimbatore outside Germany which employees close to 5500 in the city.

TRANSPORT IN TAMIL NADU

Tamil Nadu, a state in South India, has a highly developed, dense, and modern transportation infrastructure, encompassing both public and private transport. Its capital city, Chennai is well-connected by land, sea, and air and serves as a major hub for entry into South India.

Roadways

Roads in Tamil Nadu

Tamil Nadu has an extensive road network. The state road network covers about 153 km per 100 km area, which is higher than the country's average road network coverage of 103 km per 100 km area.

A separate Highways Department (HD) was established in April 1946 and the same has been renamed as Highways & Minor Ports Department (HMPD) on 30 October 2008. HMPD of Tamil Nadu is primarily responsible for construction and maintenance of roads including national highways, state highways and major district roads in Tamil Nadu.

It operates through 7 wings namely National Highways Wing, Construction & Maintenance Wing, NABARD and Rural Roads Wing, Projects Wing, Metro Wing, Tamil Nadu Road Sector Project Wing, Investigation and Designs Wing geographically spread across the state in 31 districts with about 120 divisions and 450 subdivisions.

National Highways

In Tamil Nadu, "National Highways Wing" of Highways & Minor Ports Department was established in the year 1971 to look after the works of improving, maintaining and renewing of National Highways laid down by National Highways Authority of India (NHAI).

NH 47, NH 49, NH 208 and NH 220 connects Tamil Nadu with Kerala. NH 67, NH 207 and NH 209 connects Tamil Nadu with Karnataka. NH 205, NH 219 and NH 234 connects Tamil

Nadu with Andhra Pradesh. NH 4 connects Tamil Nadu with Maharashtra, Karnataka, and Andhra Pradesh. NH 5 connects Tamil Nadu with Orissa and Andhra Pradesh. NH 7 connects Tamil Nadu with Uttar Pradesh, Madhya Pradesh, Maharashtra, Andhra Pradesh, and Karnataka. NH 66 connects Tamil Nadu with Karnataka and Puducherry.

State Highways

Roads which connects district headquarters, important towns and the National Highways in the State and neighboring States are declared as State Highways. Construction & Maintenance wing of Highways Department looks after Construction, Maintenance of all the State Highways (SH), Major District Roads (MDR), Other District Roads (ODR). Tamil Nadu State Highways Network has 7 circles namely Chennai, Coimbatore, Salem, Trichy, Madurai and Tirunelveli.

Other Roads

This category includes Major District Roads, Other District Roads (ODR), Rural & Sugarcane Roads and Special Roads such as East Coast Road, Rajiv Gandhi Salai / IT Expressway, Ennore-Manali Road Improvement Project (EMRIP), Chennai Port – Maduravoyal Expressway and Outer Ring Road Project. This Roads provides linkage between production and marketing centers within a district. It also provides connectivity for district & taluk headquarters.

The East Coast Road was the first project implemented by Tamil Nadu Road Development Company (TNRDC) in the year 2002 which runs from Chennai till outskirts of Puduchery for a total length of 113.2 kilometres (70.3 mi).

The 19 kilometres (12 mi) long Chennai Port – Maduravoyal Expressway is being developed by Chennai Port Trust and Government of Tamil Nadu on 50:50 cost sharing basis at cost of 1,655 crore (US$230 million). The 62 kilometres (39 mi) long Outer Ring Road with six lanes from Vandalur to Minjur is the project developed at a cost of 1,000 crore (US$140 million) in two phases.

Tamil Nadu Road Network

Class	Length (km)
National highways/expressways	4,873
State highways	9,384
Major district roads	11,288
Other district roads & sugarcane roads	36,096
Panchayat roads and other departments roads	1,37,399
Total (approx)	1,99,040

Public Transport

Tamil Nadu State Transport Corporation (TNSTC) is the public transport bus operator of Tamil Nadu, India. It operates buses along intra and inter state bus routes, as well as city routes. TNSTC is the largest government bus transport corporation in India. There are currently 8 divisions in TNSTC including Metropolitan Transport Corporation in Chennai and State Express Transport Corporation.

State Express Transport Corporation Limited (SETC) formerly known as Thiruvalluvar Transport Corporation runs long distance express services exceeding 250 km and above throughout the state of Tamil Nadu linking all important capital cities, historical places, religious places and commercial places etc., and adjoining states of Andhra Pradesh, Karnataka, Kerala and the Union Territory of Puducherry. SETC provides advance booking and reservation on all of its routes. SETC operates buses of various classes of services such as semi-deluxe, ultra-deluxe and air-conditioned. CMBT in Chennai, operated by transport department is one of the largest bus stations in Asia.

Private Transport

Chennai is home to around 35-40% of India's total automobile industry and hence it is known as the Detroit of Asia. It will become one of the world's largest auto hubs by 2016 with a capacity of over 3 million cars annually. Tamil Nadu has over 17.5 million registered vehicles with nearly 730% growth over the last two decades. Private bus services are operated in both short and long haul routes by mofussil bus operators.

Railways

Tamil Nadu has a good rail network as part of Southern Railway. Headquartered at Chennai, the Southern Railway network extends over a large area of India's Southern Peninsula, covering the states of Tamil Nadu, Kerala, Puducherry, a small portions of Karnataka and Andhra Pradesh.

Tamil Nadu has a total railway track length of 5,952 km (3,698 mi) and there are 532 railway stations in the state. The system connects it with most major cities in India. Main rail junctions in the state include Chennai, Madurai, Coimbatore, Erode, Tiruchirapalli and Salem.

Mass Rapid Transit System

Chennai, India's fourth-largest urban agglomeration, has a well-established suburban railway network, which dates back to 1931, when services began on the metre-gauge line from Beach to Tambaram.

The Mass Rapid Transit System (MRTS) is an elevated line of the urban mass transit system (metro-like cityrail) in Chennai (Madras), India. The line currently runs within city from Chennai Beach (Madras Beach) to Velachery, covering a distance of 25 km with 21 stations. Despite of full technical and logical separation from the Chennai Suburban Railway, the MRTS is operated by the state-owned Southern Railway (SR), a zone of Indian Railways.

Chennai Metro

The Chennai Metro is a rapid transit rail system in the Tamil Nadu capital city of Chennai. The Phase I of the project consisting of two corridors is under construction. The elevated section of the project was scheduled to be operational by 2011 and the entire project was scheduled to be completed by the financial year 2014-2015. About 55% of the corridors in Phase I is underground and the remaining elevated. The project is estimated to cost around 14,600 crore (US$3.17 billion) for the two corridors totaling 45 km.

Airways

Tamil Nadu has a major international airport Chennai International Airport, which is the fourth busiest airport by passenger traffic and is the third largest cargo hub in India.

Other international airports present in the state are Coimbatore International Airport and Tiruchirapalli International Airport.

Madurai Airport is a customs airport with limited international flights. Neyveli Airport, Salem Airport and Tuticorin Airport are domestic airports. Increased industrial activity has given rise to an increase in passenger traffic as well as freight movement which has been growing at over 18 per cent per year.

Waterways

Tamil Nadu has three major seaports at Chennai, Ennore, Thoothukudi. There are 11 other ports. Chennai Port is an artificial harbor situated on the Coromandel coast and is India's second busiest container hub, handling general industrial cargo, automobiles, etc. Ennore Port handles all the coal and ore traffic in Tamil Nadu.

ROAD NETWORK IN TAMIL NADU

In Tamil Nadu, the Highways & Minor Ports Department (HMPD) is primarily responsible for construction and maintenance of roads including national highways, state highways and major district roads. HMPD was established as Highways Department (HD) in April 1946 and subsequently renamed on 30 October 2008. It operates through seven wings namely National Highways Wing, Construction & Maintenance Wing, NABARD and Rural Roads Wing, Projects Wing, Metro Wing, Tamil Nadu Road Sector Project Wing, Investigation and Designs Wing geographically spread across the state in 32 districts with about 120 divisions and 450 subdivisions.

Road Network

As on 30 June 2018, Tamil Nadu's road network has a total road length of 199,040 km (123,680 mi). Tamil Nadu has about 17,089 km (10,619 mi) of highways which is designated as National Highways and *State Highways* on the basis of traffic intensity and connectivity. The various types of roads and their lengths are given below:

National Highways

Road stretches which have heavy traffic intensity of more than 30,000 Passenger Car Units (PCUs) connecting different state capitals, major ports, large industrial areas and tourist centers are designated National Highway by Government of India.

In Tamil Nadu, *National Highways Wing* of Highways & Minor Ports Department was established in the year 1971 to look after the works of improving, maintaining and renewing of National Highways laid down by National Highways Authority of India (NHAI).

National Highways wing exercises central government funds from Ministry of Road Transport and Highways for improvement works. Out of 25 National Highways in Tamil Nadu, 12 highways completely lie within the state. National Highways plying through Tamil Nadu are listed below in the table:

State highways

Road stretches with heavy traffic intensity of more than 10,000 PCUs but less than 30,000 PCUs which connects district headquarters, important towns and the National Highways in the State and neighboring States are declared as State Highways. Construction & Maintenance wing of Highways Department looks after Construction, Maintenance of all the State Highways (SH), Major District Roads (MDR), Other District Roads (ODR). Tamil Nadu State Highways Network has 7 circles namely Chennai, Villupuram, Madurai, Salem, Tiruchirappalli, Coimbatore, Tirunelveli.

Major District Roads

Roads with traffic density less than 10,000 PCUs but more than 5,000 PCUs are designated as Major District Roads (MDR). Major District Roads provide linkage between production and marketing centers within a district. It also provides connectivity for district and taluk headquarters with state highways and national highways. Construction and Maintenance wing of Highways Department executes construction and maintenance of MDRs along with State Highways. These roads have a minimum width of 15 metres (49 ft).

Other District Roads (ODR)

Roads with traffic density less than 5,000 PCUs are categorized as Other District Roads (ODR). ODRs provides road connectivity for major rural production hubs, blockheadquarters and taluk headquarters. Similar to SH and MDRs, Construction and Maintenance wing of Highways Department executes ODR related works.

Rural & Sugarcane Roads

NABARD and Rural Roads Wing of Highways and Minor Ports Department carry out construction and maintenance of rural roads along with Pradhan Mantri Gram Sadak Yojana. NABARD and state government shares the funds required for the development of rural roads. In 2010, NABARD sanctioned 816 crore(US$110 million) for augmentation of 508 rural roads in 30 districts, upgrading 44 district roads and 39 major district roads in 18 districts and construction of 121 bridges in 31 districts of the state.

Other Roads

East Coast Road

The East Coast Road was the first project implemented by Tamil Nadu Road Development Company (TNRDC) in the year 2002. ECR Road runs from Kudumiyandithoppu till outskirts of Pondicherry for a total length of 113 km (70 mi). Recently

Tamil Nadu Government has upgraded the ECR road till Mahabalipuram to four lanes at a cost of 672 crore (US$94 million).

Coimbatore bypass

Coimbatore Bypass is a series of bypasses connecting the various National Highways and State Highways passing through and originating in Coimbatore. The first section of the bypass was a 28-kilometre (17 mi) two-laned road with paved shoulders built by Larsen & Toubro (L&T) from Neelambur to Madukkarai on National Highway 544 (formerly National Highway 47) which intersects Trichy Road at Chintamani Pudur near Irugur and Eachanari on Pollachi Road. It was the first road privatisation project to be implemented on a build-operate-transfer model in South India. The National Highways Authority of India is conducting studies for a bypass along the Mettupalayam–Sulur National Highways 81 and 181 (formerly National Highway 67). The proposed length of this road is 53.95 kilometres (33.52 mi), and is expected to cost 6.01 billion (US$84 million) to build. In 2010, an announcement was made in the State Budget to build a Western Ring Road at a cost of 2.84 billion for 26 km. The proposed road would have been from Madukarai near ACC Cement industry, starting on Palakkad Road connecting Mettupalayam Road via Perur Road, Marudamalai Road and Thadagam Road.

IT Expressway

Road Stretch from Madhya Kailash in Adyar to Mahabalipuram in Kanchipuram district which in turn connects with the East Coast Road is called Rajiv Gandhi Salai or IT Expressway. TNRDC developed this road stretch in two phases with widening of Madhya Kailash to Siruseri road stretch to six lanes in first phase and widening of Siruseri to Mamallapuram of road stretch I second phase.

Ennore-Manali Road Improvement Project (EMRIP)

Ennore–Manali Road Improvement Project was developed by a special purpose vehicle formed by National Highways

Authority of India (NHAI), Chennai Port Trust (CPT), Ennore Port Limited (EPL) and Tamil Nadu Government (GoTN) at a cost of Rs 600 crore. The project was announced by the State Government in 1998 to cover industrial hotspots of north Chennai such as Manali Oil Refinery Road, Tiruvottiyur–Ponneri-Panchetti (TPP) Road, Ennore Expressway and northern portion of the Inner Ring Road from Madhavaram to Manali.

Chennai Port – Maduravoyal Expressway

The 19 km (12 mi) long Chennai Port – Maduravoyal Expressway is being developed Chennai Port Trust and Government of Tamil Nadu on 50:50 cost sharing basis. The 1,655 crore (US$230 million) Elevated Expressway project was awarded to Hyderabad based Soma Enterprises.

Outer Ring Road Project

The 62-km long Outer Ring Road with six lanes from Vandalur to Minjur via Nemellichery was awarded to GMR consortium by Chennai Metropolitan Development Authority to implement the project on a Design, Build, Finance, Operate and Transfer (DBFOT) basis. The project is proposed to be developed at a cost of 1,000 crore (US$140 million) in two phases. In the first phase, the 30 km (19 mi) long stretch of road from Vandalur in NH-45 to Nemellichery in NH-205 via Nazrathpet in NH4 is to be developed. The 30 km (19 mi) long stretch of road between Thiruninravur Nemellichery to Thiruvottiyur-Ponneri-Panchetti in Minjur is under construction.

Chennai Peripheral Ring Road

The proposed Chennai Peripheral Ring Road starts at Ennore port travels through the proposed Northern Port Access Road and connects Mamallapuram near Poonjeri junction of East Coast Road (ECR). The Government sanctioned Rs. 10 Crore for the preparation of Detailed Project Report (DPR) for this work and the same has been completed.

7

Tourism

TOURISM IN TAMIL NADU

Tamil Nadu is a state in the south-eastern part of the Indian Peninsula. Tamilnadu is previously a part of the United Madras Province, which was later partitioned based on languages. Tamilnadu has more than 4,000 years of continuous cultural history. Tamil Nadu has some of the most remarkable temple architecture in the country, and a living tradition of music, dance, folk arts and fine arts. Tamil Nadu is well renowned for its temple towns and heritage sites, hill stations, waterfalls, national parks, local cuisine and the natural environment and wildlife. The state has the largest tourism industry in India with an annual growth rate of 16%. In 2015, the number of domestic arrivals was at 333.5 million making the state the most popular tourist destination in the country, and foreign arrivals numbered 4.68 million, the highest in the country, making it the most popular state for tourism in the country.

Economy and Tourism

Tamil Nadu with a GDP of $150 billion is the second largest economy of the country and Tourism is one of the main sources of its revenue. Tourism in the state is promoted by the Tamil Nadu Tourism Development Corporation headquartered in the capital city of Chennai. Tamil Nadu is a year-round tourist destination, and the industry is the largest in the country.

Madurai Meenakshi Amman Temple North Tower

Major Cities of Tamil Nadu

Chennai

Chennai formerly known as Madras, is the capital city of the state, and India's fourth largest metropolis. The city is known for its beaches, ancient Tamil architecture, Anglo-Indian architecture, cultural festivals and is India's largest shopping destination. Chennai is seen as the gateway to Southern India and is well connected to all parts of India by road, rail and air.

The city is currently India's 4th largest and one of the world's fifty most largest ones. This city houses Asia's largest hospitals which has recently spurred a new wave of medical tourism.

Coimbatore

Coimbatore also called as textile city or cotton city is the second largest city in the state of Tamil Nadu. It is often referred to as the Manchester of South India due to its growing commercial importance. Coimbatore is situated in the Western end of Tamil Nadu and is well connected by road, rail and air with major towns and cities in India. Important place to visit is ISHA yoga.

Madurai

Inner view of Thirumalai Palace

Madurai is the third largest city by population in Tamil Nadu and the second largest corporation in Tamil Nadu. Madurai has been a major settlement for two millennia. Madurai was the longest continuous capital city until British rule in India, and was the first major settlement in central and southern Asia. It is one of India's temple towns. It is also called Temple city, Athens of East, City of Junctions, City of Festival, Jasmine city, Sleepless city (*Thoonga Nagaram*). The city is synonymous with Tamil Literature, Tamil was patronised by the city and vice versa. Madurai is the topmost tourism hub of Tamil Nadu. Madurai is the cultural headquarters of Tamil Nadu, Madurai is the major city to attract more Foreigners next only to Chennai. Madurai also ancient city its living civilization is more than 4000 years. While Pandiyan emperor it is the capital of Pandyan Kingdom. Madurai continues to be a cultural hot spot in the state and is a major tourist destination for overseas visitors.

Meenakshi Temple

The Sri Meenakshi temple is located in Madurai. The temple in the present form was re- constructed by the pandyas of Madurai. The temple has a 1000 pillar hall, 14 towers with remarkable art, architecture and painting. Thirugnanasambandar the Hindu Saint has mentioned the temple in his songs which go back to the early 7th century. At least 15,000 visitors visit these temples regularly which include both Indians and Foreigners. The temple is now administered by HR and CE department of Tamil Nadu.

Thirumalai Nayak Mahal

Thirumalai Nayak Mahal is located at a distance of 2 km from Meenakshi Amman Temple. The palace is a testament to the Indian art and architecture. There are 248 pillars in the palace, each 58 feet tall and 5 feet in diameter. The paintings in the palace reflect the art of painting prevailed in the 16th century. Only a part of the largest palace is allowed for site seeing. In this palace of rectangular shape, audio-visuals are shown in the evenings. The Mahal is open to general public between 9 am to 1 pm and between 2 pm to 5 pm. Sound and light show: English at 6.45 pm, Tamil will be played at 8.15 pm. The city is 450 km from Chennai and has a major railway junction and an airport 12 km from the city.

Thiruparankundram Dargah

Thiruparankundram Dargah at the top of Thiruparankundram hills the Shrine of Hazrat Sulthan Sikandar Badusha Shahhed, who came along with Badusha Sulthan Syed Ibrahim Shaheed of Erwadi. People of all faiths majorly from the neighbouring state of Kerala visit this shrine at the top of the hill. The shrine is open from 5AM till 9PM.

Kazimar Big mosque and Madurai Maqbara

Kazimar Big Mosque is the first mosque in Madurai built in the year 1284 under the supervision of Hazrat Kazi Syed Tajuddin in a land donated by the pandiya kings. Madurai

Maqbara the shrine of 3 great sufi saints of Madurai is located within the mosque.

Goripalayam dargah

Goripalayam Dargah is the tomb of the Sulthans of Madurai Hazrat Sulthan Alauddin Badusha and Hazrat Sulthan Shamsuddin Badusha. It is located in the heart of Madurai city in the northern banks of river vaigai. Madurai is well connected with major cities in India by Madurai International Airport and main railway junction Madurai Junction.

Tiruchirappalli

Tiruchirappalli also called Tiruchi or Trichy, is a city in the Indian state of Tamil Nadu and the administrative headquarters of Tiruchirappalli District. It is the fourth largest municipal corporation and the fourth largest urban agglomeration in the state. Located 322 kilometres (200 mi) south of Chennai and 379 kilometres (235 mi) north of Kanyakumari, Tiruchirappalli sits almost at the geographic centre of the state. The Kaveri Delta begins 16 kilometres (9.9 mi) west of the city as the Kaveri river splits into two, forming the island of Srirangam now incorporated into Tiruchirappalli City Municipal Corporation. Occupying 167.23 square kilometres (64.57 sq mi), the city was home to 916,674 people as of 2011.

Tiruchirappalli's recorded history begins in the 3rd century BC, when it was under the rule of the Cholas. The city has also been ruled by the Pandyas, Pallavas, Vijayanagar Empire, Nayak Dynasty, the Carnatic state and the British. The most prominent historical monuments in Tiruchirappalli include the Rockfort, the Ranganathaswamy Temple at Srirangam and the Jambukeswarar temple at Thiruvanaikaval. The archaeologically important town of Uraiyur, capital of the Early Cholas, is now a suburb of Tiruchirappalli. The city played a critical role in the Carnatic Wars (1746–1763) between the British and the French East India companies.

The most commonly used modes of local transport in Tiruchirappalli are the state government-owned Tamil Nadu

State Transport Corporation (TNSTC) buses, and auto rickshaws. Tiruchirappalli forms a part of the Kumbakonam division of the TNSTC. The city has two major bus termini; Chatram Bus Stand and Central Bus Stand, both of which operate intercity services and local transport to suburban areas.

Tiruchirappalli sits at the confluence of two major National Highways—NH 45 and NH 67. NH 45 is one of the most congested highways in south India and carries almost 10,000 lorries on the Tiruchirappalli–Chennai stretch every night. Other National Highways originating in the city are NH 45B, NH 210 and NH 227. State highways that start from the city include SH 25 and SH 62. Tiruchirappalli has 715.85 km (444.81 mi) of road maintained by the municipal corporation. A semi-ring road connecting all the National Highways is being constructed to ease traffic congestion in the city. As of 2013, approximately 328,000 two-wheelers, 93,500 cars and 10,000 public transport vehicles operate within the city limits, apart from the 1,500 inter-city buses that pass through Tiruchirappalli daily. Tiruchirappalli suffers from traffic congestion mainly because of its narrow roads and absence of an integrated bus station.

Passenger trains also carry a significant number of passengers from nearby towns. The Great Southern of India Railway Company was established in 1853 with its headquarters at England. In 1859, the company constructed its first railway line connecting Tiruchirappalli and Nagapattinam. The company merged with the Carnatic Railway Company in 1874 to form the South Indian Railway Company with Tiruchirappalli as its headquarters. The city retained the position until 1908 when the company's headquarters was transferred to Madras. Tiruchirappalli Junction is the second biggest railway station in Tamil Nadu and one of the busiest in India. It constitutes a separate division of the Southern Railway. Tiruchirappalli has rail connectivity with most important cities and towns in India. Other railway stations in the city include Tiruchirappalli Fort, Tiruchirappalli Town, Srirangam, Palakkarai and Golden Rock.

The Railway Heritage Centre was formally inaugurated on 18 February 2014, and is located adjacent to the Rail Kalyana Manadapam (Community Hall), near Tiruchirappalli Junction.

Tiruchirappalli is served by Tiruchirappalli International Airport (IATA: TRZ, ICAO: VOTR), 5 km (3.1 mi) from the city centre. It is the 10th busiest airport in the country in terms of international traffic. The airport handles fivefold more international air traffic than domestic services, making it the only airport in India with this huge variation. It serves as a gateway to immigrants from South-east Asian countries. There are regular flights to Chennai, Colombo, Dubai, Kuala Lumpur, Mumbai and Singapore. The airport handled more than 1 million passengers and 2012 tonnes of cargo during the fiscal year 2013–14.

Salem

Salem is a city of Tamil Nadu state in southern India. Salem is the district headquarters and other major towns in the city include Edappadi, Mettur, Omalur and Attur. Salem is surrounded by hills and the landscape dotted with hillocks. Salem has a vibrant culture dating back to the ancient Kongu Nadu. As a district, Salem has its significance in various aspects; it is known for mango cultivation, silver ornaments, textile, sago industries and steel production. As of 2011, the district had a population of 3,482,056 with a sex-ratio of 954 females for every 1,000 males. Salem is one of the biggest cities in Tamil Nadu. Tourist places include Yercaud, Mettur Dam, Kailasanathar Temple, Kottai Mariamman Temple. Salem is connected with other parts of Tamil Nadu and other states by road, rail and bus.

Salem's traditional shopping areas are in the Town area, with major retailers in Bazaar Street, Car Street, First Agraharam and Chinna Kadai Street. Shevapet and the Fort area are noted for hardware and furniture, and Leigh Bazaar in Shevapet is the main wholesale market. Reliance Shopping Mall, the city's largest shopping complex is situated near Five Roads. Kurumbapatti Zoological Park and Anna Park are government-run parks. Paravasa Ulagam and Dream Land are amusement parks in the city.

Salem Airport (IATA *SXV*, ICAO *VOSM*) is located on the Salem-Bangalore Highway (NH 7) in Kaamalapuram about 15 kilometres (9.3 mi) from the city. Airports Authority of India (AAI) opened the airport in 1993 for commercial operations.

Salem has six arterial roads: Omalur Road, Cherry Road, Saradha College Road, Junction Main Road, Gugai Main Road and Attur Road. Three National Highwaysoriginate in or pass through: NH 44 (Srinagar – Kanyakumari), NH 544 (Salem – Kochi via Erode and Coimbatore) and NH 79 (Salem – Ulundurpet).

Salem is the headquarters of the Salem division of TNSTC. The city has two major bus stations: the MGR Integrated Bus Terminus in Meyyanoor and the Town Bus Station (Old Bus Stand) in the town area. Intercity and interstate routes and private buses originate at the Central Bus Stand, and local buses originate at the Old Bus Stand. The Anna Flyover is the oldest in the city, and the Trumpet Interchange was built in the realignment of NH 544 to ease traffic towards Coimbatore.

Salem Junction is located in Suramangalam, 5 kilometres (3.1 mi) west of the city. In 2005, the Railway Board approved the creation of a Salem railway division from Palakkad and Tiruchirapalli divisions. It is the fourth-largest of the six Southern Railway zone divisions. Salem Railway Junction has been rated as the most clean station among the divisional headquarters railway stations and also the ninth cleanest railway station in the entire country, according to a survey report published in June 2017.

Erode

Erode ([i□ro}o□]) is the administrative headquarters of Erode District in the South Indian state of Tamil Nadu. Located on the banks of River Kaveri, and has been ruled, at different times, by the Early Pandyas, Medieval Cholas, Later Cholas, Vijayanagar Empire, Madurai Nayaks, Hyder Ali, Carnatic kingdom, and the British. It is situated at the center of the South Indian Peninsula, about 400 kilometres (249 mi) southwest of the state capital Chennai and about 80 kilometres (50 mi) east of Coimbatore.

Hand loom, power loom textile products and ready made garments industries contribute to the economy of the city. The people in the city are employed in various textile, oil and turmeric manufacturing industries.

Being the district headquarters, Erode accommodates the district administration offices, government educational institutes, colleges and schools.

Erode is a part of Erode constituency (Erode East and Erode West) and elects its member of legislative assembly every five years, and a part of the Erode constituency that elects its member of parliament. The city is administered by a municipal corporation established in 2009 as per the Municipal Corporation Act. The city covers an area of 8.99 km and had a population of 173,600 in 2001. The provisional population totals of the 2011 census indicate the population of the city is 521,776. Roadways is the major mode of transport to the city, while it has also got rail connectivity. The nearest airport is Coimbatore International Airport, located at a distance of 90 km from the city.

Vellore

Vellore is a city and the administrative headquarters of Vellore District in the South Indian state of Tamil Nadu. It is on the banks of Palar River and has been ruled, at different times, by the Pallavas, Medieval Cholas, Later Cholas, Vijayanagar Empire, Rashtrakutas, Carnatic kingdom, and the British. It is about 145 kilometres (90 mi) west of the state capital Chennai. Vellore has historic Vellore Fort and buildings, Government Museum, Science Park, Religious Places like Jalakandeswarar Temple, Srilakshmi Golden Temple, Big Mosque and St. Johns church, Amirthi Zoological Park and Yelagiri Hill station are the among top tourist attractions in and around Vellore City.

Thoothukudi

Thoothukudi is a commercial city on the sea shore which serves the inland cities of Southern India and is one of the sea gateways of Tamil Nadu. There are stretches of sunny and sandy beaches that are restful and calm. There are several towns that have historical and religious significance that are around Thoothukudi. It has a railway terminus and a domestic airport with regular flights to Chennai.

Tirunelveli

Tirunelveli is an ancient city and is home to many temples and shrines, including the largest Shiva temple in Tamil Nadu, the Nellaiappar Temple. It is located on the western side of the perennial Thamirabarani river, whereas its twin municipal city Palayamkottai, is located on the eastern side. It has a major railway junction and is situated 700 kilometres southwest of the state capital, Chennai.

UNESCO World Heritage Sites

The state houses a no. of heritage sites mainly composed of the ancient temples and deities of the Pallava and Chola empire scattered along various parts of Northern and Central-Eastern parts of Tamil Nadu. The following are the list of the Heritage sites in the state.

The Chola Temples

The Great Living Chola Temples constructed by the king Raja Raja Chola and his son Rajendra are part of the Cultural heritage site which includes the three great temples of 11th and 12th century namely, the Brihadisvara Temple at Thanjavur, the Brihadisvara Temple at Gangaikondacholisvaram and the Airavatesvara Temple at Darasuram.

- Thanjavur - The home to the Chola Kingdom and the location of the Brihadisvara Temple built in the 11th Century.

A Dravidian architecture Pillar in Airavatesvara Temple, Darasuram @ Thanjavur district.

- Gangaikonda Cholapuram - The capital of the Chola kingdom for 250 years.
- Darasuram - A small town close to Kumbakonam, the town has the prestigious Airavatesvara Temple dedicated to Lord Shiva along with the Brihadeeswara Temple and the temple of the Gangaikonda Cholapuram are three of the most venerated and architectural legacies of the Chola empire.

The Airavatesvara Temple at Darasuram, an 11th-century temple dedicated to Lord Shiva.

Group of Monuments in Mahabalipuram

The Group of Monuments at Mahabalipuram declared as a World Heritage Site in 198, in Tamil Nadu, about 58 km from Chennai, were built by the Pallava kings in the 7th and 8th centuries. The town is said to have gained prominence under the rule of Mamalla. These monuments have been carved out of rock along the Coromandel coast. The following are the sites related. These monuments surprisingly survived the 2004 Tsunami that devastated the other coastal towns nearby.

- Ratha Temples: Temples in the form of chariots.
- The 11 Mandapas: Cave sanctuaries dedicated to various deities.
- Rock Reliefs that include Descent of the Ganges and the Arjuna's Penance.
- The Shore Temple and the other temples cut out of rock.
- The Seven Pagodas

Karaikudi

Karaikudi is the famous heritage site of Tamil Nadu for its culture and its state or art architecture.

The Nilgiri Mountain Railway

Part of the Mountain railways of India, the Nilgiri Mountain Railway(NMR) was stated to be an "outstanding examples of bold, ingenious engineering solutions for the problem of establishing an effective rail link through a rugged, mountainous terrain." The Nilgiri Mountain Railway was added to the list in 2005 preceding the Kalka-Shimla Railway which was granted the status in 2008.

The Route passes through the various terrains and thickly forested areas of the Nilgiri Mountains. The route consists of the following stations:

- Mettupalayam
- Kaalar
- Hillgrove
- Runneymede
- Kateri Road
- Coonor
- Wellington
- Aruvankadu

- Ketti
- Lovedale
- Ooty

RELIGIOUS SITES OF TAMIL NADU

Tamil Nadu has the credit of having 34000 Hindu temples some of which are several centuries old. The cities in ancient Tamil Nadu is believed to have revolved around the magnificent temples built by the Pallava, Chola and Pandya empires and therefore most of the cities in the state have a lot of religious significance and contain a number of temples and shrines in and around their limits. Temple towns like Madurai and Kanchipuram are thronged by visitors throughout the year.

Caves

Kalugumalai

Kalugumalai Jain Beds

Kalugumalai consist of three important Temples in Kalugumalai:

- Kalugumalai Jain Beds : There are many rock relief sculptures dating to the 8th-9th century A.D. in the area, including the rock cut image of Bhagawan Parshwanatha flanked by two Yaksha, as well as many other rock cut images of other tirthankaras. The sculptures and the epigraphs are to be assigned to the reign of Pandya, Parantaka Nedunjadaiya (A.D. 768-800). There are approximately 150 niches in the bed, that includes images of Gomateshwara, Parshvanatha and other Tirthankaras of the Jainism. The Jain beds are maintained and administered by Department of Archaeology of the Government of Tamil Nadu as a protected monument.

Vettuvan Koil

- Vettuvan Koil : is a Hindu temple built between the 8th and 9th century. Kalugumalai is a priceless unfinished Pandyanmonolith cave temple, part of the iconographic richness that helped chronicle the burgeoning richness of the Tamil culture, traditions, and sacred centres containing religious art. The temple is carved out from a single rock in a rectangular portion measuring 7.5 m (25 ft) in depth. The carvings in the temple show the top portion of the temple, with an unfinished bottom. The granite rock looks like a blooming lotus, with hills surrounding it on three sides. The vimana (ceiling over the sanctum) has niches of Parsavadevatas, the attendant deities of Shiva, like ganas, Dakshinamurthy depicted playing a mridanga, Siva with his consort Uma, dancers, various niches of Nandi (the sacred bull of Shiva) and animals like monkeys and lions.

- Kalugasalamoorthy Temple : The main deity of this temple is Murugan. The main deity hall and entrance hall is excavated inside the foot hills of kalugumalai in the south western corner of the hill and with external structural additions. The temple has many aesthetic sculptures.The temple dates to the 18th century.

Chitharal Jain Monuments

Chitharal Jain Monuments or Chitharal Malai Kovil are situated on the Thiruchanattu Malai (Thiruchanattu hillocks) near Chitharal village, Kanyakumari district, Tamil Nadu, India. There are two monuments. The earlier rock-cut Jain structure of beads with inscriptions and drip-ledges is the earliest Jain monument in the southernmost part of India which was from first century BC to sixth century AD. The temple monuments were likely built by Digambara Jains in the ninth century when the region was under influence of Jainism. Jain influence in this region was due to the King Mahendravarman I (610-640).

Sittanavasal Cave

The Sittanavasal Cave is a rock-cut monastery or temple. Created by Jains, it is called the Arivar Koil, and is a rock cut cave temple of the Arihants. It contains remnants of notable frescoes from the 7th century. The murals have been painted with vegetable and mineral dyes in black, green, yellow, orange, blue, and white. Paintings have been created by applying colours over a thin wet surface of lime plaster. Temple-cave was initially dated to Pallava King Mahendravarman I (580–630 AD) prior to his conversion from Jainism to Hinduism as a Shaivite. However, an inscription attributes its renovation to a Pandyan king probably Maran Sendan (654–670 AD) or Arikesari Maravarman (670–700 AD).

Sittanavasal is a rock-cut cave, situated on the western side of central part of a hill, which runs in a north-south direction. The hill measures approximately 70 metres (230 ft) in height, and sits above the surrounding plain which has some archaeological monuments. The Jain natural caverns, called Ezhadippattam are approached from the foothills. The cave is approached by climbing a few 100 steps.

The architectural features of the Sittanvasal Cave include the painting and sculptures found within its precincts.Archaeological Survey of India is responsible for the maintenance of the cave and the Jain beds.

Samanar Hills

Samanar Hills or Samanar Malai is a hill rock complex located in Keelakuyilkudi village, 15 kilometres (9.3 mi) from Madurai, Tamil Nadu, India.

Samanar Malai has several Tamil-Brahmi inscriptions, a number of stone beds and many sculptures, which shows authority for Jainism in the ancient Tamil country. The hill contains two noted sculptures, *Settipodavu* and *Pechipallam*, that show images of Jain Tirthankaras made by Jain monks in the 9th century BCE. The *Settipodavu* contains the image of Mahavira, the last tirthankara of Jainism. The *Pechipallam* contains eight sculptures, including Bahubali and Mahavira.

More than 2000 years old Tamil-Brahmi inscriptions and Vatteluttu writings.

Temples, Mosques and Churchs

Velankanni

Velankanni is located 12 km south of Nagapattinam on the Eastern coast. The town is home to a significant Roman Catholic shrine dedicated to Our lady of Good Health. Virgin Mary is believed to have miraculous healing powers. In 1560, Virgin Mary is said to have appeared to a shepherd, asking him for milk to quench the thirst of baby Jesus. When the shepherd returned to his master, after performing the good deed, his pitcher kept filling up with milk. Consequently, a small thatched chapel was built at the site. At the end of the 16th century, Virgin Mary appeared again in front of a lame boy, who regained the use of his limbs. The actual church was constructed after the incident.Thus, the Pope in the Vatican City has declared Velankanni as a Holy City. Thousands of pilgrims belonging to various castes and communities flock daily to this 'Lourdes of the East'.

Chidambaram

Chidambaram is the seat of the cosmic dancer Lord Nataraja (Ananda Tandava pose ; the Cosmic Dance of bliss). It is one of the Pancha Bhutasthalas. The Chidambaram Temple dedicated to Lord Natraja built in the 9th century has an unusual hut-like sanctum with a gold-plated roof and four towering gopuras. Many Chola kings were crowned here in the presence of the deity. Nearby a sculptural temple is Melakadambur, with its distinct architecture that makes it resemble a chariot.

Ervadi

Erwadi is a small town in Ramanathapuram district which houses the 840-year-old shrine and the graves of Hazrat Sulthan Syed Ibrahim Shaheed badusha and the graves of a few thousands of His friends, family and followers who came from Saudi Arabia in the mid 12th century. The site is well known for its spiritual healing for mental and magical diseases.Kattupalli, Meesal, Natham (Keelakarai), Sundaramudayan, Thachu oorani, Vaippar and Valinokkam are some notable shrines within the district and near by. The Annual Santhanakoodu festival held during the Islamic month of Dhul Qidah is very well recognized and witnessed by more than 1 million people from different region and of all faiths.

Kancheepuram

One of the most visited destinations in the state, Kanchipuram was the capital of the ancient Pallava Kingdom and is considered one of the seven holiest cities to the Hindus of India. Hundreds of ancient temples are located in this town, though most of them are in ruins, there are a few prominent ones which attract a large number of devotees every year.

The Kailashnathar Temple dedicated to Lord Shiva is the oldest temple of Kanchi. It reflects the grandeur and the splendor of the early Dravidian style of temple architecture built by the Pallava king Rayasimha.

This temple was constructed in the late seventh century AD and the eighth century remains of murals within the temple are an indication of the magnificence of the original temple that was supposed to exist much before than the temple today. The Ekambareswarar Temple built by the Pallavas and extended by the Cholas is another popular temple in the town sprawling over a large area of 12 hectares.

The Kamakshi Amman Temple dedicated to Goddess Parvati is the main pilgrimage center in the town and one of the three temples of worship of Goddess Parvati in Tamil Nadu. The Trilokyanatha Temple is a Jain temple built by King Simhavishnu is dedicated to Mahavira.

The Varadharaja Perumal Temple, the Devarajswmi Temple and the Pandava Thoothar Perumal Temple are the other major temples in the environs.

Kanniyakumari

The southernmost tip of the subcontinent, Kanniyakumari is known for the Hazrat Peer Mohammed waliyullah Dargah, Kumari Amman Temple and the Thanumalayan Temple. Other religious sites include the Mondaicaud Bhagavathi Temple, Sri Adikesavaperumal Temple, St. Xavier's Church, devasahayam mount, St. Therese of Infant Jesus church and the St. Arockiya Nathar Church within the district..

Kumbakonam

Kumbakonam, 40 km from Thanjavur, has about 188 temples within its municipal limits. Apart from these a thousand more are estimated to be nearby. The Adi Kumbeswarar Temple is the biggest Saivite temples in the region and has a huge complex covering an area of 30,181 sq ft having three gopurams in the Northern, Eastern and Western entrances of the temple.

After the Adi Kumbeshwara Temple, the second most important landmark s the Ramaswamy Temple dedicated to Lord Rama from the epic of Ramayana and has a no. of intricate crvings within its pillars depicting the various scenes of the epic.

The Kashi Vishwanath Temple here is another example of ancient Dravidian architecture in the region. The tank of the temple contains the waters of the 9 holy rivers in Hindu mythology namely Ganga, Yamuna, Narmada, Saraswati, Kaveri, Godavari, Tungabhadra, Krishna and Sarayu and a no. of pilgrims visit this temple on the Mahamaham festival once in 12 years to bathe in the waters of the tank which they believe would purify them from their sins.

The Sarangapani Temple is one of the five most important Vaishanavaite pilgrimage centres in South India and had the tallest Gopuram in the region before the Temple town of Srirangam was built. To the south of the temple is the Someswar Templeanother flagship of Dravidian architecture.

Madurai

Madurai also called as "Temple city" . Madurai consists of major temples. Madurai being one of the world's oldest inhabited cities is the home to several temples built by the Pandyan and Nayak kings, including the Meenakshi Amman Temple which dates back to 2000 years.

The city and the life of its inhabitants revolve around the temple which is one of the largest Hindu temples by size and enclosure. Every year, hundreds of thousands of tourists visit this temple and the surroundings.

The Mariamman Theppakulam built in 1636 is a huge tank at the eastern end of the city and is almost equal in area to that of the Meenakshi Amman temple. To its side is a temple dedicated to Parvati, and every year a local festival celebrating Goddess Meenakshi's wedding is held in the month of January/ February.

Madurai is also situated close to the Thirupparamkunram Murugan Temple and Pazhamudircholai, two of the Six Abodes of Lord Subramanya.

Thiruparankundram Dargah at the top of Thiruparankundram hill is a well-known Islamic shrine. Madurai is also known for its two mosques one being the Kazimar Big Mosque constructed by Kazi Syed Tajuddin, a descendant of Prophet Muhammed the oldest Islamic monument in Madurai. Madurai Maqbara the dargah of 3 Shadhuli Sufi saints is located within the mosque. The other is the Goripalayam Mosque the tombs of two of the Delhi Sultans.

Nagore

Nagore, a town north of Nagapattinam, is the home to the tomb of Meeran Sahib Abdul Qadir Shahul Hamid Badshah also known as the Nagore Durgah a spiritual place for all faiths. The Durgah as it stands now was built by devotees whose wishes were fulfilled by praying Shahul. It is believed that 60 percent of the shrines were built by Hindus and there are other shrines built in his honour in Penang(Malaysia) and Singapore. The urs festival celebrated every year draws Hindus and Muslims from all over the world.

Palani

The largest pilgrimage center in Tamil Nadu and the second largest in South India after Tirupati, Palani is the most famous of the Six Abodes of Murugan (Arupadai Veedu Temple Tour). During the Thai Poosam festival, the temple attracts over 7 million devotees, many of whom do a lot of penances and acts such as shaving their heads, walking barefoot all the way from their homes etc. to show their devotion. A cable-car service ferries devotees to the top of the hill. Palani is also a base for hikes in the surrounding hills. A railway station links the town to Coimbatore and Madurai.

Rameshwaram

Ramanathaswamy Temple at Rameswaram

Situated at the tip of the Pamban Island and 50 km from the coast of Sri Lanka, is considered to be as sacred as Varanasi and is a bustling pilgrimage center. Named after Lord Rama who according to the Legend embarked his journey to Sri Lanka from this town, Rameshwaram is a place of wide religious significance. The city is one of the holiest Hindu Char Dham shrines that has to be visited in one's lifetime and this island Temple is connected by the scenic Pamban Bridge over the sea for 2.3 km.

The Ramanathaswamy Temple, the most important of them all is believed to be constructed at the spot where Lord Rama had offered his prayers to Shiva. The construction of the temple as it stands today, was started in the 12th century and ended in the 19th century. The most interesting feature in the temple is the 1,220m long corridor (the longest in India) with carvings on its pillars, walls and ceiling.

The Kothandaramaswamy Temple situated on the shore of Dhanushkodi is supposed to be the place where Vibishena the brother of Raavana, had met Rama's army and joined hands. The temple miraculously survived the 1964 Cyclone that destroyed most of the region and receives a good number of visitors.

The village of Devipatinam 20 km from Ramnathapuram has a temple dedicated to Lord Jagannatha and about hundred yards in the sea are naturally existing nine blocks of stone, supposed to be the Navagrahas, the nine planets.

Srirangam

Srirangam another example of classic temple town, houses the Ranganathaswamy Temple a major pilgrimage destination for the Vaishnava community. It is the biggest functioning Hindu temple in the world (156 acres) and the temple tower measuring 60 m (196 ft) is the tallest Hindu temple tower in the world.

East of the Rangnathasamy temple is the 17th-century temple town of Jambukeshvar Temple, in the town of Tiruvanaikka an important destination for worshipers of Lord Shiva.

Thiruvannamalai

In Arunachaleshwara Temple of Thiruvannamalai, Siva is worshipped in the form of fire. The temple town of Thiruvannamalai is one of the most ancient heritage sites of

India and is a centre of the Saiva religion. The Arunachala hill and its environs have been held in regard by the Tamils for centuries. The temple is grand in conception and architecture and is rich in tradition, history and festivals. The main Deepam festival attracts devotees from far and wide throughout South India. A number of spiritual centres are also located in the region:

- Sri Seshadri Swamigal Ashram:It was created by the Mahan Sri Seshadri Swamigal lived in the late 20th Century.. People from all over the world visit this Ashram, which is situated near the Sri Ramana Ashram.
- Sri Ramana Ashram: Mahan Ramana Maharshi lived in Thiruvannamalai town. Sri Ramana Ashram is one the holy places in this town. People from throughout the globe visit this Ashram. He attained mukthi in the year 1950.
- Yogi Ram Surathkumar Ashram: Yogi Ram Surathkumar Ashram, also known as Visiri Samiyar Ashram, is situated near the Ramana Ashram. He attained mukthi/salvation in the year of 2000.

Tirumalai

Tirumalai is an ancient Jain temple complex in the outskirts of Tirvannamalai that houses three Jain caves, four Jain temples and a 16 feet (4.9 m) high sculpture of Neminatha dated from the 12th century and the tallest Jain image in Tamil Nadu. Temple is famous for paintings that have been added to the site between the 15th-17th centuries. Arahanthgiri Jain Math is a Jain Mathathat was established near the site in August, 1998.

Thiruvarur

Sri Thyagaraja Temple is a Hindu temple dedicated to Lord Thyagaraja located in the town of Tiruvarur in Tamil Nadu, India. The temple is revered by the Thevaram hymns of Saiva nayanars, 7th century Tamil saint poets and classified as Paadal Petra Sthalam. The temples complex occupies an area of around

33 acres with the Kamalalayam tank to its west. There are numerous shrines and mandapas(halls) in the three spacious enclosures(prakaram). The two main shrines of the temple are for Valmikinathar(Lord Siva) and Thyagarajar.

Sri Thyagaraja Temple

Of the two, the former is the most ancient, and derives its name from tha anthill(putru), which takes the place of linga in the main shrine. Appart, the 7th-century poet saint, refers to the main deity in his hymn as puttritrukondan (one who resides in the ant hill). The Stala vriksham (temple tree) is patiri (trumpet flower tree). The principles and practises of tree-worship and ophilotary are ancient bases whereupon a later date linga worship seems to have been established.[1] Here all the 9 Navagrahams located towards south in straight line also located in northwest corner of 1st (prakaram). This temple hold the record of having maximum sannithis in India. The temple hosts the annual car festival in March for ten days. Animated crowd push and pull the largest temple car of Tamil Nadu and its smaller cars on the laborious path around the surrounding streets.

Tiruchendur

Another of the Six Abodes, the Thiruchendur Murugan Temple located here attracts hundreds of thousands of devotees. The temple is situated so close to the sea that waves from the Gulf of Mannar lap at the eastern perimeter wall of the temple. The temple however had no damage done by the 2004 tsunami.

The other temples in the town and its neighbourhood are:

- Sri Ponvandu Aiyanar temple, at the hamlet called Nainarpattu.
- Sri Karkuvel Aiyanar temple, at the hamlet called Theri Kudiirruppu near Kayamozhi.
- A temple to Arunchunai Kattha Aiyanar Swami is located at a nearby natural spring called "Sunai".
- Nallur Thirunageshwaramudayar with the Aramvalartha Nayagi Sivan temple. An old temple, the Santhana Mariyamman temple, is also nearby. This Ambal is a fertility shrine.
- A thousand-year-old Sri Somanatha temple is situated at Authoor, 18 km from Thiruchendur.
- Kulasekaranpatinam, a village 13 km away, is known for its Dasara festival. The village has the only temple where Muthu Aara Amman / Muthu Maalai Amman (Aaram and Maalai means garland in Tamil language) is shown with his consort.
- Located about 10 km from Thiruchendur, the village of Melaputhukudi is considered a holy place because of its ancestral Aiyanar temple, which includes a thalamboo grove, which is popular as a picnic

Tiruchirapalli

Tiruchirapalli,it is also a known temple city of Tamil Nadu. Tiruchirappalli (Trichy, in short) is nicknamed as "ROCK FORT CITY". Trichy has many temples in and around the city. The 'Ucchi Pillayar' shrine located at the top of the prominent ruins of the Rock Fort is the popular temple in the city. Tiruchirapalli is also very close to the Parvati temple in Samayanallur and the temple towns of Srirangam and Tiruvanaikkaval.

Srirangam is famous for its Sri Ranganathaswamy Temple, a major pilgrimage destination for Hindus (including Srivaishnavites) and the largest temple complex in India.

According to the temple's website, Srirangam can be considered the biggest functioning Hindu temple in the world, as it covers an area of about 631,000 square metres (6,790,000 sq ft) with a perimeter of 4 km (10,710 ft). Angkor Wat is bigger but non-functioning.

Srirangam is the foremost of the eight self-manifested shrines (Swayam Vyakta Kshetras) of Lord Vishnu. It is also considered the first, foremost and the most important of the 108 main Vishnu temples (Divyadesams). This temple is also known as Thiruvaranga Tirupati, Periyakoil, Bhoologa Vaikundam, Bhogamandabam. In the Vaishnava parlance the term "KOIL" signifies this temple only. The temple is enormous in size. The temple complex is 156 acres (0.63 km2) in extent. It has seven prakaras or enclosures. These enclosures are formed by thick and huge rampart walls which run round the sanctum. There are 21 magnificent towers in all prakaras providing a unique sight to any visitor. The temple town lies on an islet formed by the twin rivers Cauvery and Coleroon.

The Srirangam temple complex is composed of 7 concentric walled sections and 21 towers gopuram. The gopuram of the temple is called the Rajagopuram and is 236 feet (72 m) tall, the tallest in Asia. The temple has seven prakaras (elevated enclosures) with gopurams articulating the axial path, the highest at the outermost prakara and the lowest at the innermost. In historic times, just after the construction of this temple, the city of Srirangam lived completely within the walls of this temple and hence is quoted as an example of Hindu religious utopia - during its peak of existence.

The Srirangam temple is one of the three temples of the god Ranganata that are situated in the natural islands formed in the Kaveri river. They are:

Adi Ranga: the Ranganathaswamy temple at Srirangapattana

Madhya Ranga: the Ranganathaswamy temple at Shivanasamudra

Antya Ranga: the Ranganathaswamy temple at Srirangam

There is a gopuram fully made of gold, which is protected by electrical fence.

Clothes such as Silk Sarees, Dhoti, Towels, etc.., used for religious purposes are auctioned here.

Inside the temple compound, there is a separate temple for the goddess Andal. Additionally, There is a museum, a library and a bookshop as well.

Thiruvanaikaval(Thiru+Aanai+kaval) or Thiruvanaikoil is a suburb of the city of Tiruchirappalli in Tamil Nadu, India. It is situated on the northern banks of the Kaveri river adjacent to Srirangam Island. The island [Thiruvanaikaval-Srirangam] is surrounded by river kaveri (southern) and river kollidam (northern), The Kollidam is the northern distributary of the Kaveri River. The Jambukeswarar Temple is located here. The temple's presiding deity is Lord Shiva (Jambukeswara) and the goddess is Sree Akilandeswari. It is revered as one of the Pancha-Bhoota Stalams (Water).There is a fresh water spring underneath the Shiv Linga. Sree Adi Shankara is said to have visited this shrine and has done the Thadanga (Ear Rings) Pratishta for the goddess to ensure that she remains in a Sowmya Roopa. It is also the birthplace of the world-renowned Nobel Laureate C. V. Raman .

Ucchi Pillayar koil, is a 7th-century Hindu temple, one dedicated to Lord Ganesh located a top of Rockfort, Trichy, Tamil Nadu, India. Mythologically this rock is the place where Lord Ganesh ran from King Vibishana, after establishing the Ranganathaswamy deity in Srirangam.

Samayapuram Mariamman Temple is a Hindu temple in Samayapuram near Tiruchirappalli in Tamil Nadu, India. The main deity, Samayapurathal or Mariamman is made of sand and clay like many of the traditional Mariamman deities, and hence unlike many other Hindu deities there are no abhishekams (sacred washing) conducted to the main deity, but instead the "abishekam" is done to the small stone statue in front of it.

It is believed by the devotees that the Goddess has enormous powers over curing illnesses and hence, it is a ritual to buy small metallic replicas, made with silver or steel, of various body parts that need to be cured, and these are deposited in the donation box.

Devotees also offer mavilakku, a sweet dish made of jaggery, rice flour and ghee. Offerings of raw salt is also made to the Goddess by the rural devotees.

The temple attracts thousands of devotees on Sundays, Tuesdays and Fridays, the holy days for Mariamman. Samayapuram is the second most wealthy (in terms of cash flows) temple in Tamil Nadu after Palani.

Dhyanalinga

Dhyanalinga is a yogic temple located at the Velliangiri Mountains, 30 kilometers from Coimbatore. The temple was created by Sadhguru, founder of Isha Foundation, and is dedicated as a meditative space. It is maintained in total silence. The linga is 13 feet 9 inches in height, and is one of the tallest lingas in the world. It is said to contain all seven chakras in an energized form.Around 600,000 devotees visit the temple on Maha Shivaratri day. Near the Dhyanalinga is the Linga Bhairavi temple, dedicated to the mother goddess, Linga Bhairavi. The devi is uniquely in the form of a linga.

The Dhyanalinga premises are also the location of the 112-foot Adiyogi statue, which was inaugurated by the Prime Minister of India, Narendra Modi, on Maha Shivaratri, 2017. The statue represents Shiva as the Adiyogi or first yogi, and the Adi Guru or first Guru, who offered yoga to humanity. It is the tallest bust of Shiva in the world. The height of the statue - 112 feet - represents the 112 ways Adiyogi is said to have offered, in which a human being can attain mukti.

Hill Stations

Tamil Nadu situated in the southern end of the Western and Eastern ghats is the home to several hill stations. Popular among them are Udagamandalam(Ooty), Kodaikanal, Yercaud, Coonoor, Valparai, Yelagiri, Sirumalai, Kalrayan Hills and the Kolli Hills. The Nilgiri hills, Palani hills, Shevaroy hills and Cardamom hills are all abodes of thick forests and wildlife.

Udagamandalam

Houses in Ooty

Popularly known as Ooty situated in the Nilgiri Biosphere Reserve is the most popular Hill station in South India. It provides a scenic view of Nilgiri Hills. The town is connected to the rest of India by road and the popular Nilgiri Mountain Railway, and its historic sites and natural environment attract tourists from all over the country. The list of attractions include:

- Government Rose Garden – The largest Rose garden in India.
- Ooty Lake
- St. Stephen's Church
- Ooty Golf Course

- Tribal Museum
- Doddabetta Peak
- Wenlock Downs
- Emerald and Avalanche Lakes
- Pykara Falls

Kodaikanal

Located in the forests of the Dindigul districts, the hill station of Kodaikanal is fast gaining reputation for its "unspoilt beauty and soothing climate". It is known by the nickname "Princess of Hill stations" and is a leading tourist destination in Tamil Nadu. The most popular sights within the town are:

- The Kodaikanal Lake – Kodaikanal's most popular geographic landmark and tourist attraction. Rowboats and pedalos can be hired at the Kodaikanal Boat Club. Very popular with tourists.
- Bryant Park: Just east of the lake is the Bryant Park. Over 325 species of trees, shrubs and cacti and flowers.
- Coaker's Walk – A paved pedestrian path offering stunning views of the mountains and the plains below.
- Green Valley View – Offers views of the plains and the Vaigai River Dam at the South.
- Shembaganur Museum of Natural History – A nature museum with over 500 species of local wildlife and 300 exotic orchid species.
- Silver Cascade – A waterfall in the region popular with first-time visitors.
- Berijam Lake – A calm lake surrounded by nature.

Valparai

Valparai is a Taluk and hill station in the Coimbatore district of Tamil Nadu, India. It is located 3,500 feet above sea level on the Anaimalai Hills range of the Western Ghats, at a distance of 100 kilometres from Coimbatore. The tea plantations are surrounded by evergreen forest. The region is also a rich elephant tract and is known to have many leopards.

The drive to the town from Pollachi passes through the Indira Gandhi Wildlife Sanctuary noted for elephants, boars, lion-tailed macaques, gaur, spotted deer, sambar, and giant squirrels. The area is also rich in birds, including the great hornbill. Water bodies at Monkey Falls and Aliyar Dam are also seen en route. Valparai receives among the highest rainfall in the region during the monsoons (around June).

The Valparai range is also habitat to the Nilgiri tahr, an endemic wild ungulate. These mountain goats inhabit the high ranges and prefer open terrain, cliffs and grass-covered hills, a habitat largely confined to altitudes from 1200 to 2600m in the southern Western Ghats.

Meghamalai

Meghamalai, popularly called High Wavy Mountains, is a cool and misty mountain range situated in the Western Ghats in Theni district, Tamil Nadu. It is dotted with cardamom plantations and tea estates. The place is situated at an elevation of 1,500 m above sea level and it is rich in flora and fauna. This area, now mostly planted with tea, includes Cloudlands, Highwavys and Manalaar estates, the access to which is now largely restricted. It still includes large untouched remnants of evergreen forest.

Yercaud

The Yercaud hills situated at an altitude of 1515 m in the Salem District is an enchanting and picturesque hill station in the Eastern Ghats. Known for its rich flora and scenic views of the other hills, nearby Yercaud receives a good number of tourists every year for its slightly less-expensive fare as compared to Udagamangalam or Kodaikanal. Yercaud is also a great base for trekking and visiting neighbouring tourist spots like:

- Killiyur Falls – a 27-metre-high waterfall.
- Lady's seat – a high peak offering views of the plains below.

- The Servaroyan Temple – The temple is a narrow and dark cave having the God Servarayan and the Goddess Kaveri inside, which are believed as the deities of the Shevaroy Hills and Cauvery River.
- Pagoda Point: Another vantage view point; once adorned with stone built pagodas, it is now home to a large temple.
- Heaven's Ledge: A Scenic west-facing cliff situated in Gowri Estate in Yercaud. It has been converted into a campsite to encourage sustainable tourism. It is 15 km from the main town area.

Kolli Hills

Kolli Hills is a small mountain range located in central Namakkal District of Tamil Nadu in India. The mountains are relatively untouched by commercial tourism and still retain their natural beauty. The government holds a tourism festival in August. Kolli Hills has been the top choice for nature lovers, hiking enthusiasts, trekking clubs and meditation practitioners among hill stations in Tamil Nadu. Kolli hills is less polluted and mostly unexplored compared to the other hill stations in the state and effective steps re being implemented to improve the area as to make it more tourist-friendly. Kolli Hills has been the top choice for nature lovers, hiking enthusiasts, trekking clubs and meditation practitioners among hill stations in Tamil Nadu. In comparison to other hill stations in Tamil Nadu, Kolli Hills is not commercialized, less polluted and offers unique mountain ranges. Agaya Gangai is a waterfall situated near the Arappaleeswarar temple. Additionally the district administration has recently developed a botanical garden, Boat house, Cave house, New waterfalls called Masila Falls. The administration also celebrated "Ori festival" with lot of cultural events

Coonoor

Part of the Nilgiri Mountain Range, Coonoor is the second largest hill station in the mountain range and is an ideal base for trekking expeditions leading into the Nilgiri Mountains.

Coonor is en route the Mettupalayam-Ooty highway as well as the NMR and is an ideal break-point for tourists to Ooty. The Dolhin's Nose Viewpoint and the Lamb's Rock offer stunning views of the mountainside. The attractions in the town and nearby include -

- Sim's Park – The main attraction within the town, a small well maintained botanical garden that has several varieties of plants. An annual fruit show is held in the town in summer.
- Droog Fort – At a distance of 13 km from Coonoor, the Droog takes one into the past, with the ruins of a fort, which was once used by Tipu Sultan in the 18th century.
- Law's Falls
- Catherine Falls
- Sri sathya sai baba temple of 20 km from coonoor located at Mel-hosahatty village.
- sri Shiridi sai baba temple of 8 km from coonoor located at yedappalli village.

Waterfalls—Courtallam

Courtallam Falls, popularly referred to as the Spa of South India

Courtallam, the 'Spa of the south', is situated at an elevation of about 167m on the Western Ghats in Tirunelveli District. It is an excellent health resort and is visited by young and old alike, because of the herbal medicinal properties the water is believed to contain. The town is noted for its salubrious climate and natural scenery.

Hogenakkal falls

Hogenakkal waterfalls located close to the border of the adjacent state of Karnataka in the district of Dharmapuri. It is a picnic spot with its waters supposed to be having curative powers. Hogenakkal is set in thick, green woods and is considered both a sacred bathing place and a spa-like health resort. Here the water spreads for miles around. The area is surrounded by hills and offers lovely panoramic view. People can take bath in the Kaveri river, before and beyond the falls. Tamil Nadu Forest Department recently launched Hogenakkal Eco Tourism website to offer ecotourism activities, accommodation, and trekking near Hogenakkal.

Agaya Gangai falls

Agaya Gangai waterfalls are located in Kolli Hills of the Eastern Ghats. Panchanathi, a jungle stream, cascades down as the *Agaya Gangai* (En:Ganges of Sky), near the Arapaleeswarar temple atop the Kolli Hills in Namakkal district, Tamil Nadu. It is a 300 feet (91 m) waterfall of the river Aiyaru situated close to Arapaleeswarar temple. It is located in a valley that is surrounded by mountains on all sides. The caves of Korakka Siddhar and Kalaanginatha Siddhar are situated near the Agaya Gangai waterfalls inside the forest area

Catherine falls

Catherine Falls is a double-cascaded waterfall located in Kotagiri(near Coonor), The Nilgiris District, Tamil Nadu and It is also a major tourist spot in Kotagiri. It is on the Mettupalayam road branching off at Aravenu. The upper fall drops to the floor, and is the second highest in the Nilgiri mountains. It can clearly been seen from the top of Dolphin's

Nose if seeing the entire waterfall as one total impression is what you are looking for.

Kiliyur falls

Kiliyur Falls is a waterfall in the Shervaroyan hill range in the Eastern Ghats and is a popular tourist attraction in Yercaud. The waters overflowing the Yercaud Lake fall 300 ft (91 m) into the Kiliyur Valley.

Suruli falls

The Suruli Falls is a two-stage cascading waterfall from the Meghamalai mountain range. This falls is mentioned in the ancient Tamil epic, Silappathikaram. Near Suruli Falls are 18 caves which represent Indian rock-cut architecture of the 18th century. The Tamil Nadu Tourism Department celebrates summer festival at Suruli falls every year. Near to it another falls is also there, which is produced from the Princess of hills Kodaikanal. And the falls is named as Kumbakarai, nearest to Periyakulam. It is exactly 45km away from Suruli falls.

Tirparappu waterfalls

Tirparappu Waterfalls are located in Kanyakumari district. The Kodayar River makes its descent at Thiruparappu. The water fall at this place is about 13 kilometres (8.1 mi). from Pechiparai Dam. The river bed is rocky and about 300 feet (91 m) in length. The water falls from a height of nearly 50 feet (15 m) and the water flows for about seven months in a year. The whole bed above the falls is one rocky mass which extends 250 metres (820 ft) upstream where the Thirparappu weir has been constructed for supplying water to the paddy fields. On either side of the river, on the left bank of the river in between the waterfalls and the weir, there is a temple dedicated to Siva enclosed by strong fortification.

Beaches

Marina Beach

Marina Beach one of the world's longest and largest urban

beaches, is located on the eastern side of Chennai, adjoining the Bay of Bengal. Watching the sun set and rise from the beach is an enthralling experience. Second largest beach in the world. With its natural sandy and spacious promenade and gardens, the beach is an attraction for tourists visiting Chennai. The Marina, however, is large enough to accommodate all visitors as well as the hawkers and is often the venue for important state functions.

Elliot Beach

This beach is located in Besant Nagar. Formerly a popular bathing beach, today, it is the favourite rendezvous of the younger generation. Good roads, pavements, illuminated sands, makes a visit to this beach a real pleasure.

Mahabalipuram

Mamallapuram, 58 km south of Chennai, has a beach spanning a distance of over 20 km. Once the site of the erstwhile Pallava Kingdom's seaport, the place today abounds with stone carvings, caves, rock-cut temples also attract tourists. A crocodile farm, snake venom extracting centre, schools of art and sculpture and a wide choice of resorts along the beach draw holiday-seekers all round the year.

Kushi/Ariyamaan Beach

Ariyaman Beach is situated on the side of the Palk Bay in the Ramanathapuram District. The Ariyaman Beach also features children's park, watch tower and water-based attractions like wind surfing and water scooters. Tourists can also visit the aquarium and museum near the beach. This clean beach features large casuarina trees that provide shade for rest or picnic.

The beach is located at a distance of 27 km from the city and measures around 150 metres in width. It extends to a stretch of 2 km and offer boating facility and much more to tourists. Parasailing is a common activity at this beach, which is done using a parachute. This parachute takes the adventurers

200 metres above the water level and is controlled by a moving boat.

Poompuhar Beach

Once a legendary port city with trade links to ancient Greece and Rome, today Poompuhar is a small coastal town with a superb shoreline that attracts a number of tourists for its vistas during sunrise.

Kanniyakumari

Located at the southernmost tip of India, where the Arabian Sea, the Indian Ocean and the Bay of Bengal meet, lies the Kanyakumari Beach, an important pilgrim center. Kanniyakumari is known for its spectacular sunrises and sunsets, especially on full moon days. The beach itself has multi-coloured sand. There are also other beaches in Kanyakumari like Chothavilai Beach, Circular Fort.

Mangrove Forest

Pichavaram Mangrove Forest

Pichavaram (MadBoon) has a well-developed mangrove forest. Pichavaram consists of a number of islands interspersing a vast expanse of water covered with green trees. The area is about 1100 hectare and is separated from the sea by a sand bar.

The Pichavaram mangrove biotope, consisting of rare species like Avicennia and Rhizophora presents a special attraction, with its peculiar topography and environmental condition. It supports the existence of many rare varieties of economically important shell and finfishes.pichavaram mangrove forest is located between two prominent estuaries, the Vellar estuary in the north and Coleroon estuary in the south.

The Vellar-Coleroon estuarine complex forms the Killai backwater and Pichavaram mangroves. The backwaters are interconnected by the Vellar and Coleroon river systems and offer abundant scope for water sports such as rowing, kayaking and canoeing. There are more than 400 water routes available for boating.

Wildlife sanctuaries and National parks

Arignar Anna Zoological Park

Arignar Anna Zoological Park (abbreviated AAZP), also known as the Vandalur Zoo, is a zoological garden located in Vandalur, a suburb in the southwestern part of Chennai, Tamil Nadu, about 31 kilometres (19 mi) from the city centre and 15 kilometres (9.3 mi) from Chennai Airport.

It is India's largest zoo in terms of area covering 1,300 acres. Its previous location was set up in 1855 and was the first public zoo in India. It is affiliated with the Central Zoo Authority of India.[8] Spread over an area of 602 hectares (1,490 acres), including a 92.45-hectare (228.4-acre) rescue and rehabilitation centre, the park is the largest zoological garden in India.

The zoo houses 2,553 species of flora and fauna across 1,265 acres (512 ha). As of 2012 the park houses around 1,500 wild species, including 46 endangered species, in its 160 enclosures.[9] As of 2010, there were about 47 species of mammals, 63 species of birds, 31 species of reptiles, 5 species of amphibians, 25 species of fishes, and 10 species of insects in the park.[10] The park, with an objective to be a repository of the state's fauna, is credited with being the second wildlife sanctuary in Tamil Nadu after Mudumalai National Park.

Mudumalai National Park

Mudumalai which translates into "Ancient Hill Range" is situated at the base of the Nilgiri Hills, is the home to several endangered and vulnerable species such as the Nilgiri Tahr, Indian elephant, Tiger, Gaur, Flying Squirrel, Sambar, Nilgiri langur and Indian Leopard to name a few. It shares its borders with Kerala and Karnataka and is separated from Karnataka's Bandipur National Parkby the Moyar river.

The lowest point of the sanctuary is the picturesque Moyar Waterfalls. Its rich topography is as varied as the vegetation, which ranges from dense deciduous forests in the west to scrub jungles in the east interspersed with grasslands, swamps and bamboo brakes.

Mukurthi National Park

Mukurthi National Park protected area located in the western corner of the Nilgiris Plateau west of Ootacamund hill station in the northwest corner of Tamil Nadu state in the Western Ghats mountain range of South India.

The park was created to protect its keystone species, the Nilgiri tahr.The park is characterised by montane grasslands and shrublands interspersed with sholas in a high altitude area of high rainfall, near-freezing temperatures and high winds.

It is home to an array of endangered wildlife, including royal Bengal tiger and Asian elephant, but its main mammal attraction is the Nilgiri tahr.

The park was previously known as Nilgiri Tahr National Park. The park is a part of Nilgiri Biosphere Reserve, India's first International Biosphere Reserve. As part of the Western Ghats, it is a UNESCO World Heritage Site since 1 July 2012

Vedanthangal Bird Sanctuary

This is a major Forest Tourist Attraction known as water-bird sanctuary, located not far from Chennai. Vedanthangal Bird Sanctuary is a 30-hectare protected area located in the Kancheepuram District of the state of Tamil Nadu, India.

The sanctuary is about 75 kilometres from Chennai on National Highway 45, south of Chengalpattu. The best time to go is October-March, when cormorants, herons, ibis, storks, pelicans and other birds migrate here. Accommodation is available at the Forest Department Rest house.

Anaimalai Tiger Reserve

The Steering Committee of Project Tiger granted approval in principle to inclusion of Indira Gandhi WLS and NP under Project Tiger in 2005. IGWS was declared a Project Tiger sanctuary in 2008. Continuance of Project Tiger' in Anaimalai Tiger Reserve for FY 2010/11, at the cost of Rs. 23547,000, was approved by the National Tiger Conservation Authority on 31 August 2010.

This tiger reserve, together with the several other contiguous protected forest and grassland habitats, is the core of the Parambikulum-Indira Gandhi tiger habitat landscape complex, with tiger occupancy area of about 3,253 km

Sathyamangalam Tiger reserve

This tiger reserve was formed as 42nd tiger reserve of the country and houses 55 tigers. This tiger reserve has the largest population of elephants in the state. This is the largest wildlife sanctuary of Tamilnadu.

The tiger reserve offers wild safari to visitors. The visitors can see many wild animals (depending upon the season), as well as the Moyar river and the green Talamalai plateau. It is located about 70 km from Coimbatore

The Gulf of Mannar Marine National Park

The Gulf of Mannar Marine National Park is a protected area of India consisting of 21 small islands (islets) and adjacent coral reefs in the Gulf of Mannar in the Indian Ocean. It lies 1 to 10 km away from the east coast of Tamil Nadu, South India for 160 km between Thoothukudi and Dhanushkodi. It is the core area of the Gulf of Mannar Biosphere Reserve which includes a 10 km buffer zone around the park, including the populated coastal area. The park has a high diversity of plants and animals in its marine, intertidal and near shore habitats. Public access inside the Park is limited to glass bottom boat rides

Guindy National Park

Originally a part of the private forest reserve surrounding the Guindy Lodge in the suburbs of Chennai, a portion of it was declared as the Guindy National Park in 1977 and is one of the very few national parks situated within a metropolis.

The park is the home to the endangered Blackbuck and the Spotted deer and has over 130 varieties of birds including raptors such as the honey buzzard and the white-bellied sea eagle. Bird-watching is popular in winter, when migrant birds visit the region. Also located within the park is the Snake Park where one can see the King Cobra, the Python among other reptiles.

For ex-situ conservation, about 22 acres (8.9 ha) of the Guindy National Park has been carved out into a park known as the Children's Park and play area at the northeast corner of the national park with a collection of animals and birds. The park attracts more than 700,000 visitors every year.

8

Population and Religion

POPULATION OF TAMIL NADU 2018

Tamil Nadu is one of the stunning states of India. Its capital as well as the biggest city is Chennai. It lies in the southern piece of the Indian Peninsula and is bordered by Puducherry and states like, Karnataka, Kerala and additionally Andhra Pradesh. The state is bounded by the Eastern Ghats, Anamalai Hills and by the Indian Ocean. It furthermore confers a maritime border with Sri Lanka. Tamil Nadu incorporates different spots to visit and they extend from Chennai, Ooty, Mahabalipuram and so forth. The state has its very own enchant with a great deal of things to offer for its visitors.

Tamil Nadu as a state is well known for its various kinds of Thali food. It comprises of different types of flavors and things specially to suit your taste buds. The thali is easily available in all kinds of restaurants in all over the state.

Population Of Tamil Nadu In 2018

Tamil Nadu is the seventh most crowded state in India. 48.4% of the state's population lives in urban places, the most elevated among large states in the country.

Talking about population, in order to check out the population of Tamil Nadu in 2018, we need to have a look at the population of the past 5 years. They are as per the following:

1. 2013 – 74.3 Million
2. 2014 – 75.4 Million
3. 2015 – 76.6 Million
4. 2016 – 77.8 Million
5. 2017 – 79.788 Million

Predicting the 2018 population of Tamil Nadu is not easy but we can get the idea after analysing the population from the year 2013 – 17. As we have seen that every year the population increases by approximate 1.0976 Million people. Hence, the population of Tamil Nadu in 2018 is forecast to be 79.788 Million + 1.0976 Million = 80.8856 Million. So, the population of Tamil Nadu in the year 2018 as per estimated data is 80.8856 Million.

Tamil Nadu Population 2018 –80.8856 Million. (estimated).

Demography Of Tamil Nadu

Tamil Nadu comprise of 51,837,507 literates, touching the literacy rate 80.33%. There are a total of 27,878,282 laborers, incorporating 4,738,819 cultivators, 6,062,786 plant laborers and others. As per the religious insights of 2011, it had 86% Hindus, 5.9% Muslims, 6.1% Christians and 0.3% expressed no religion.

Population Density And Growth Of Tamil Nadu

The population density is 555 persons per square kilometre. The census demonstrated that the number of people in Tamil Nadu grew by 15.6% when contrasted with 11.7% in the prior decade. In any case, the country's general growth rate in the midst of the latest decade was 17.7%. In Tamil Nadu the growth of population among Hindus and Muslims was prominently lower than the national average of 16.% and 24.5%. Christians had a growth rate of 16.4% in the state.

The not so surprising growth is of Kancheepuram region, which has recorded a high decade development with 39% population settling in the area due to land costs currently.

Facts About Tamil Nadu:

1. Tamil Nadu has a transport system that interfaces all over the state by methods of roadways, rail and flight courses. Chennai has the International plane terminal yet it has diverse air terminals in Salem, Tiruchirapally and so on.
2. Well known festivals are Pongal, Thirunaal, Deapavali, Good Friday, Eid-ul-Fitr and so forth.
3. The greater part of the overall public in the State follows Hinduism with a bigger piece of 88.3%. Remaining others follow Christianity, Islam and others.
4. Chennai was previously known as Madras and is its Capital. Moreover, Chennai is the biggest city of Tamil Nadu.
5. The state is ranked 11th in terms of area.

DEMOGRAPHICS OF TAMIL NADU

According to the 2011 census, the total population stood at 72,147,039, with 36,137,975 males, 36,009,055 females, a sex ratio of 996 females per 1000 males, literacy rate of 80.09%, 10.51% of the population below seven years and a population density of 555.

Distribution of population across districts

As per details from Census 2011, Tamil Nadu has population of 72.1 million, an increase from figure of 62.4 million in 2001 c.

2011 Census

According to 2011 Census the following table represents the total, male and female population of Tamil Nadu in each district:

Important facts

Growth rate

The officially recorded growth rate of Tamil Nadu according to 2011 census is 15.61%.

Literacy

Tamil Nadu has performed reasonably well in terms of literacy growth during the decade 2001–2011. The state's literacy rate increased from 73.47% in 2001 to 80.09% in 2011.

Sex ratio

The officially recorded sex ratio is 996 females per 1000 males, which is well above the national average.

Caste demographics

As per the 2011 Census of India, Scheduled Castes and Scheduled Tribes accounted for 20.01 percent and 1.10 percent of Tamil Nadu's 72 million population. The Other Backward Classes (OBCs) formed 68% of the state's population.

Religion Data

The following table shows the total number of people belonging to each religion in Tamil Nadu:

Note: The data displayed on the page will be according to the parameters selected for viewing.

Religion	**Population**
Hinduism	63,188,168
Christianity	4,418,331
Islam	4,229,479
Jainism	89,265
Buddhism	11,186
Sikhism	14,601
Others	7414
Religion not stated	188,586
Total	more than 7 crores

Workforce

According to the 2001 census, the total number of workers in Tamil Nadu amounts to 27,878,282 with the Work

Participation rate being 44.67%. The total number of non-workers amounts to 34,527,397 or 55.33% of the population.

RELIGIONS IN TAMIL NADU

The history and culture of Tamilnadu goes back to thousands years back. For centuries, people of various religions have been residing in the state. The main religions in Tamilnadu are Hinduism, Islam, Christianity and Jainism. Hinduism, along with its various sects, is the oldest religion in the state. Hindus are followers of number of sectarian monastic institutions (called mathas). The most important Math of the state is the Shankara Math at Kumbakonam. The Hindus number most and are scattered in almost all parts of the state. In Tamilnadu, there is an established caste system, which is more pronounced than many other parts of the country. Like most parts of India, the Brahmin community in Tamilnadu is very pious. Besides Hinduism, other important religions that are practiced in the state are Christianity, Islam and Jainism. The history of Christianity and Islam is also very old in Tamil Nadu. The largest concentration of Christians is in Tirunelveli and Kanniyakumari districts of the state. The followers of Jain religion are confined to North and South Arcot and Chennai city.

HINDUISM IN TAMIL NADU

Hinduism in Tamil Nadu dates back to 5th century BC finding literary mention in Sangam literature. The total number of Tamil Hindus as per 2011 Indian census is 63,188,168 which forms 87.58% of the total popualation of Tamil Nadu. Hinduism is the largest religion of Tamil Nadu.

The religious history of Tamil Nadu is influenced by Hinduism quite notably during the medieval century. The twelve Azhwars (saint poets of Vaishnavite tradition) and sixty-three Nayanars (saint poets of Shaivite tradition) are regarded as exponents of the *bhakti* tradition of Hinduism in South India. Most of them came from the Tamil region and the last of them lived in the 9th century CE.

There are quite some worship forms and practices in Hinduism that are specific to Tamil Nadu. There are lot of Mathas (meaning monastic institutions) and temples based out of Tamil Nadu.

In modern times, most of the temples are maintained and administered by the Hindu Religious and Endowment Board of the Government of Tamil Nadu.

History

Prehistory

Tolkappiyam, possibly the most ancient of the extant Sangam works, dated between the 3rd century BCE and 5th century CE glorified Murugan, the favoured god of the Tamils."

Medieval Period (600–1300)

The Cholas who were very active during the Sangam age were entirely absent during the first few centuries. The period started with the rivalry between the Pandyas and the Pallavas, which in turn caused the revival of the Cholas. The Cholas went on to becoming a great power. Their decline saw the brief resurgence of the Pandyas. This period was also that of the re-invigorated Hinduism during which temple building and religious literature were at their best.

The Cheras ruled in southern India from before the Sangam era (300 BCE – 250 CE) over the Coimbatore, Karur, SalemDistricts in present-day Tamil Nadu and present day Kerala from the capital of Vanchi Muthur in the west, (thought to be modern Karur).

The Kalabhras, invaded and displaced the three Tamil kingdoms and ruled between the third and the seventh centuries CE of the Sangam period. This is referred to as the Dark Age in Tamil history and Hinduism in Tamil Nadu. They were expelled by the Pallavas and the Pandyas in the sixth century. During Kalabhras' rule Jainism flourished in the land of the Tamils and Hinduism was suppressed. Because the Kalabhras gave protection to Jains and perhaps Buddhists, too, some have concluded that they were anti-Hindu, although this latter view is disputed.

Meenakshi Amman Temple in Madurai built by the Pandyans.

During the fourth to eighth centuries century CE, Tamil Nadu saw the rise of the Pallavas under Mahendravarman I and his son *Mamalla* Narasimhavarman I.Pallavas ruled a large portion of South India with Kanchipuram as their capital. Mahendra Varman was principally a Buddhist, but converted to Hinduism by the influence of Saivite saints. It was under him that Dravidian architecture reached its peak with the Pallava built Hindu temples. Narasimhavarman II built the Shore Temple which is a UNESCO World Heritage Site.

The Pallavas were replaced by the Cholas as the dominant kingdom in the 10th century C.E and they in turn were replaced by Pandyas in the 13th century CE with their capital as Madurai. Temples such as the Meenakshi Amman Temple at Madurai and Nellaiappar Temple at Tirunelveli are the best examples of Pandyan temple architecture.

Chola Empire

By the 9th century CE, during the times of the second Chola monarch Aditya I, his son Parantaka I, Parantaka Chola II itself the Chola empire had expanded into what is now interior Andhra Pradesh and coastal Karnataka, while under the great Rajaraja Chola and his son Rajendra Chola, the Cholas rose as a notable power in south Asia.

The Cholas excelled in building magnificent temples. Brihadeshwara Temple in Thanjavur is a classical example of the magnificent architecture of the Chola kingdom. Brihadshwara temple is an UNESCO Heritage Site under "Great Living Chola Temples." Another example is Annamalaiyar Temple located at the city of Tiruvannamalai and the Chidambaram Temple in the heart of the temple town of Chidambaram. With the decline of the Cholas between 1230 and 1280 CE, the Pandyas rose to prominence once again, under Maravarman Sundara Pandya and his younger brother, the celebrated Jatavarman Sundara Pandyan. This revival was short-lived as the Pandya capital of Madurai itself was sacked by Alauddin Khalji's troops under General Malik Kafur in 1316 CE.

Vijayanagar and Nayak period (1336–1646)

These Muslim invasions triggered the establishment of the Hindu Vijayanagara Empire in the Deccan. It eventually conquered the entire Tamil country (c. 1370 CE). This empire lasted for almost two centuries till the defeat of Vijayanagara in the Battle of Talikota in 1565. Subsequent to this defeat, many incompetent kings succeeded to the throne of Vijayanagara with the result that its grip loosened over its feudatories among whom the Nayaks of Madurai and Tanjore were among the first to declare their independence, despite initially maintaining loose links with the Vijayanagara kingdom." As the Vijayanagara Empire went into decline after mid-16th century, the Nayak governors, who were appointed by the Vijayanagar kingdom to administer various territories of the empire, declared their independence. The Nayaks of Madurai and Nayaks of Thanjavur were most prominent of them all in the 17th century. They reconstructed some of the oldest temples in the country such as the Meenakshi Temple.

Rule of Nawabs, Nizams and British (1692–1947)

In the early 18th century, the eastern parts of Tamil Nadu came under the dominions of the Nizam of Hyderabad and the Nawab of the Carnatic. While Wallajah was supported by the English, Chanda Shahib was supported by the French by the middle of the 18th century. In the late 18th century, the western parts of Tamil Nadu, came under the dominions of Hyder Ali and later Tipu Sultan, particularly with their victory in the Second Anglo-Mysore War. After winning the Polygar wars, the East India Company consolidated most of southern India into the Madras Presidency coterminous with the dominions of Nizam of Hyderabad. Pudukkottai remained as a princely state. The Hindu temples were kept intact during this period, and there is no notable destruction recorded.

Tamil Nadu in independent India (1947 -)

When India became independent in 1947, Madras Presidency became Madras State, comprising present day Tamil Nadu, coastal Andhra Pradesh, South Canara district Karnataka, and parts of Kerala. The state was subsequently split up along linguistic lines. In 1969, Madras State was renamed Tamil Nadu, meaning *Tamil country*.

The total number of Tamil Hindus as per 2011 Indian census is 63,188,168 which forms 87.58% of the total popualation of Tamil Nadu.

Hindus in Tamil Nadu (2001 census)

Parameter	**Population**
Total Population	54985079
Literates Population	35011056
Workers Population	25241725

Cultivators Population	4895487
Agricultural Workers Population	8243512
HH Industry Workers Population	1330857
Other Workers Population	10771869
Non-Workers Population	29743354

Saints

The twelve Azhwars (saint poets of Vaishnavite tradition) and sixty-three Nayanmars (saint poets of Shaivite tradition) are regarded as exponents of the *bhakti* tradition of Hinduism in South India. Most of them came from the Tamil region and the last of them lived in the 9th century CE. Composers of Tevaram - the Tamil saint poets of 7th century namely Appar, Tirugnana Sambandar and Sundarar with the 9th-century poet Manickavasagar, the composer of Tiruvacakam were saints of Shaivism. The saivite saints have revered 276 temples in Tevaram and most of them are in Tamil Nadu on both shores of river Cauvery. Vaippu Sthalangal are a set of 276 places having Shiva temples that were mentioned casually in the songs in Tevaram. The child poet, Tirugnana Sambandar was involved in converting many people from Buddhism and Jainism to Hinduism. The saint Appar was involved in *Uzhavatru padai*, a cleaning and remodification initiative of dilapidated Shiva temples. The Azhwars, the 12 vaishnavite saint poets of 7th-9th century composed the Divya Prabandha, a literary work praising god Vishnu in 4000 verses.

The development of Hinduism grew up in the temples and mathas of medieval Tamil Nadu with self-conscious rejection of Jain practises.

Monastic institutions

Smartha (Vedic)

The Smartha or the Aryan ritualistic form of Brahminical Hinduism was introduced into the Tamil lands closer to the 5-6th century AD, it soon became the standard form of Hinduism in the Tamil country and was propagated as such by the different ruling dynasties in Tamil Nadu, the Shaivate and Vaishnavate moments started as a result of this introduction. The Kanchi Matha serves as the foremost smartha institution in the state, Kanchi Matha's official history states that it was founded by Adi Sankara of Kaladi, and its history traces back to the fifth century BCE. A related claim is that Adi Sankara came to Kanchipuram, and that he established the Kanchi mutt named "Dakshina Moolamnaya Sarvagnya Sri Kanchi Kamakoti Peetam" in a position of supremacy (Sarvagnya Peetha) over the other mathas of the subcontinent, before his death there. Other sources give the place of his death as Kedarnath in the Himalayas.

Shaivate

Madurai Adheenam is the oldest Saivite Matha in South India established around 600 CE by saint Campantar. It is located two blocks from the huge Madurai Meenakshi Amman Temple, one of the most famous Siva-Shakthi shrines in the world. It is an active centre of *Saiva Siddantha* philosophy. It is currently headed by Sri Arunagirinatha Gnanasambantha Desika Paramacharya. The adheenam is the hereditary trustee of four temples in Thanjavur District.

Thiruvaduthurai Adheenam is a mutt based in the town of Thiruvaduthurai in Kuthalam taluk of Nagapattinam District, Tamil Nadu, India. As of 1987, there were a total of 15 Shiva temples under the control of the adheenam.

Dharmapuram Adheenam is a mutt based in the town of Mayiladuthurai, India. As of 1987, there were a total of 27 Shiva temples under the control of the adheenam.

Vaishnavite Matha

Parakala Mutt was the first monastery of the Sri Vaishnava sect of Brahmin Hindu society. The Mutt was first established by Brahmatantra Swatantra Jeeyar, a disciple of SriVedanta Desika by 1268 A.D. The Mutt got the name "Parakala" by the grace of Tirumangai Alvar also known as Parakalan. The head of this Matha is the heredetary Acharya of the Mysore Royal Family. The Hayagriva idol worshipped here is said to be handed down from Vedanta Desika.

Ahobila Mutt (also called Ahobila Matam) is a Vadakalai Sri Vaishnava religious institution established 600 years ago at Ahobilam in India by Athivan Satakopa Svami (originally known as Srinivasacharya). Athivan Sathakopa, a Vadakalai Brahmin, who was a great grand disciple of *Vedanta Desika* and a sishya of *Brahmatantra Swatantra Jiyar of Parakala Mutt*, founded and established the Muth, based on the Pancharatra tradition. Since then a succession of forty-six ascetics known as *"Azhagiya Singar"* have headed the monastic order.

Worship forms

Hinduism is a diverse system of thought with beliefs spanning monotheism, polytheism, panentheism, pantheism, monism, atheism, agnosticism, gnosticism among others; and its concept of God is complex and depends upon each individual and the tradition and philosophy followed. It is sometimes referred to as henotheistic (i.e., involving devotion to a single god while accepting the existence of others), but any such term is an overgeneralization.

The major worship forms of Shiva temples are for Shiva, Parvathi, Ganesha and Muruga. Vishnu is either worshipped directly or in the form of his ten avatara, most famous of whom are Rama and Krishna.

Lingam

The Lingam is a representation of the Hindu deity Shiva used for worship in Hindu temple. The *lingam* is the principal deity in most Shiva temples in South India. The propagation of *linga* worship on a large scale in South India is believed to be from Chola times (late 7th century A.D.), through Rig veda, the oldest literature details about worshipping Shiva in the form of *linga*. Pallavas propagated Somaskanda as the principal form of worship, slightly deviating from the *Shaiva agamas*;

Cholas being strict *shaivas*, established *lingams*in all the temples.

Decorated form of Shiva Lingam

Pillayar (Tamil)/ Ganesha

Ganesha, also spelled Ganesa or Ganesh, also known as Ganapati, Vinayaka and Pillaiyar (Tamil: "), is one of the deities best-known and most widely worshipped in the Hindu pantheon.Ganesa is the first son of Shiva and is given the primary importance in all Shiva temples with all worship starting from him. Local legend states the Tamil word Pillayar splits into *Pillai* and *yaar* meaning who is this son, but scholars believe it is derived from the Sanskrit word *pulisara* meaning elephant. K. A. Nilakanta Sastri (1963:57-58) thinks that Pallavas adopted the Ganesa motif from Chalukyas. During the 7th century, Vatapi Ganapati idol was brought from Badami (Vatapi - Chalukya capital) by Paranjothi, the general of Pallavas who defeated Chalukyas. In modern times, there are separate temples for Ganesha in Tamil Nadu.

Murugan

Image of Skanda, the six faced God

Murugan also called Kartikeya, Skanda and Subrahmanya, is more popular in South India especially among Tamil people famously referred as *Thamizh Kadavul* (God of Tamils). He is the patron deity of the Tamil land (Tamil Nadu). *Tolkappiyam*, possibly the most ancient of the extant Sangam works, dated between the 3rd century BCE and 5th century CE glorified Murugan, " the red god seated on the blue peacock, who is ever young and resplendent," and " the favoured god of the Tamils.". The Sangam poetry divided space and Tamil land into five allegorical areas and according to the Tirumurugarruppatai (circa 400-450 A.D.) attributed to the great Sangam poet Nakkiirar, Murugan was the presiding deity of the Kurinci region (hilly area). *Tirumurugaruppatai* is a deeply devotional poem included in the ten idylls (Pattupattu) of the age of the third Sangam. The cult of Skanda disappeared during the 6th century and was predominantly expanded during late 7th century Pallava period - Somaskanda sculptured panels of the Pallava period stand as a testament.

Lingothbhavar

Lingothbhavar or emergence of *linga*, found in various puranas as a symbol of Shiva, augments the synthesis of the old cults of pillar and phallic worship. The idea emerged from deity residing in a pillar and later visualised as Shiva emerging from the *lingam* The *lingothbhavar* image can be found in the first precinct around the sanctum in the wall exactly behind the image of Shiva. Appar, one of the early *Saivite* saint of the 7th century, gives evidence of this knowledge of *puranic* episodes relating to *Lingothbhavar*form of Shiva while Tirugnana Sambandar refers this form of Shiva as the nature of light that could not be comprehended by Brahma and Vishnu.

Nataraja

Nataraja or Nataraj, *The Lord (or King) of Dance*; (Tamil: " (Kooththan)) is a depiction of the Hindu god Shiva as the cosmic dancer Koothan who performs his divine dance to destroy a weary universe and make preparations for god Brahma to start the process of creation. A Tamil concept, Shiva was first depicted as Nataraja in the famous Chola bronzes and sculptures of Chidambaram. The dance of Shiva in Tillai, the traditional name for Chidambaram, forms the motif for all the depictions of Shiva as Nataraja.The form is present in most Shiva temples in South India, and is the main deity in the famous temple at Chidambaram.

Dakshinamurthy

Dakshinamurthy

Dakshinamurthy or Jnana Dakshinamurti is an aspect of Shiva as a guru (teacher) of all fields. This aspect of Shiva is his personification of the ultimate awareness, understanding and knowledge. The image depicts Shiva as a teacher of yoga, music, and wisdom, and giving exposition on the shastras (vedic texts) to his disciples.

Somaskandar

Somaskanda derives from Sa (Shiva) with Uma (Parvathi) and Skanda (child Murugan). It is the form of Shiva where he is accompanied by Skanda the child and Paravati his consort in sitting posture. Though it is a Sanskrit name, it is a Tamil concept and Somaskandas are not found in North Indian temples. In the Tiruvarur Thygarajar Temple, the principal deity is Somaskanda under the name of Thyagaraja.All temples in the Thygaraja cult have images of Somaskandar as Thyagarajar - though iconographically similar, they are iconologically different. Architecturally when there are separate shrines dedicated to the *utsava*(festival deity) of Somaskanda, they are called Thyagaraja shrines. Unlike Nataraja, which is a Chola development, Somaskanda was prominent even during the Pallava period much earlier to Cholas. References to the evolution of the Somaskanda concept are found from Pallava period from the 7th century A.D. in carved rear stone walls of Pallava temple sanctums. Somaskanda was the principal deity during Pallava period replacing *lingam*, including the temples at Mahabalipuram, a UNESCO world heritage site. But the cult was not popular and Somaskanda images were relegated to subshrines. Sangam literature does not mention Somaskanda and references in literature are found in the 7th century *Tevaram*.

Bhairavar

Bhairava is one of the eight forms of Shiva, and translation of the adjectival form as "terrible" or "frightful". Bhairava is known as Vairavar in Tamil where he is often presented as a Grama Devata or folk deity who safeguards the devotee on all eight directions. In Chola times Bhairava is referred as Bikshadanar, a mendicant, and the image can be found in most Chola temples.

Vishnu

Vishnu and his consort Lakshmi are represented in various forms or *avatars* in Vishnu temples in Tamil Nadu. The most common forms are Rama and Krishna.

Village deities

Ayyanar is worshipped as a guardian deity predominantly in Tamil Nadu and Tamil villages in Sri Lanka. The earliest reference to *Aiynar-Shasta* includes two or more hero stones to hunting chiefs from the Arcot district in Tamil Nadu. The hero stones are dated to the 3rd century C.E. It reads "Ayanappa; a shrine to Cattan." This is followed by another inscription in Uraiyur near Tiruchirapalli which is dated to the 4th century C.E. Literary references to *Aiyanar-Cattan* is found in Silappatikaram, a Tamil Jainism work dated to the 4th to 5th century C.E. From the Chola period (9th century C.E) onwards the popularity of *Aiyanar-Shasta* became even more pronounced.

Madurai Veeran is a Tamil folk deity popular in southern Tamil Nadu. His name was derived as a result of his association with the southern city of Madurai as a protector of the city.

Kali is the Hindu goddess associated with power, shakti. Kâlî is represented as the consort of Shiva, on whose body she is often seen standing. She is associated with many other Hindu goddesses like Durga, Bhadrakali, Sati, Rudrani, Parvati and Chamunda. She is the foremost among the Dasa Mahavidyas, ten fierce Tantric goddesses.

Muneeswarar is a Hindu god. 'Muni' means 'saint' and 'iswara' represents 'Shiva'. He is considered as a form of Shiva, although no scriptural references have been found to validate such claims. He is worshiped as a family deity in most Shaivite families.

Karuppu Sami (also called by many other names) is one of the regional Tamil male deities who is popular among the rural social groups of South India, especially Tamil Nadu and small parts of Kerala. He is one of the 21 associate folk-deities of

Ayyanar and is hence one of the so-called Kaval Deivams of the Tamils.

Sudalai Madan or Madan, is a regional Tamil male deity who is popular in South India, particularly Tamil Nadu. He is considered to be the son of Shiva and Parvati. He seems to have originated in some ancestral guardian spirit of the villages or communities in Tamil Nadu, in a similar manner as Ayyanar.

Caste

A steeply classified class structure existed in Tamil Nadu from around 2000 years because of the correlation in the form of cultivation, population and centralization of political system. These classes in turn are grouped into social groups especially in rural areas. The shape of class system in rural Tamil Nadu has changed dramatically because of land reform acts like 'Green Revolution'. As per 2001 census, there was a total of 11,857,504 people in Scheduled castes (SC) constituting 19 percent of Tamil Nadu and 7.1 percent of SC population in India. Leaving 840 in Buddhism and 837 in Sikhism, leaving the remaining 11855827 in Hinduism. The literacy rate (who can read, write and understand) among these stands at 63.2 percent which is lower than the 73.5 state level literacy rate.

Self-Respect Movement

The Self-Respect Movement is a movement with the aim of achieving a society where backward castes have equal human rights, and encouraging backward castes to have self-respect in the context of a caste based society that considered them to be a lower end of the hierarchy. It was founded in 1925 by Periyar E. V. Ramasamy (also known as Periyar) in Tamil Nadu, India. A number of political parties in Tamil Nadu, such as Dravida Munnetra Kazhagam (DMK) and All India Anna Dravida Munnetra Kazhagam (AIADMK) owe their origins to the Self-respect movement, the latter a 1972 breakaway from the DMK. Both parties are populist with a generally social democratic orientation.

Caste based political parties

Caste based political parties were not successful during the 1960s to late 80s when the Indian National Congress, Dravida Munnetra Kazhagam and Anna Dravida Munnetra Kazhagam were dominant. These parties emerged during the late 80s and three of the parties emerged prominent - Pattali Makkal Katchi (Pattali Makkal Katchi) among Vanniyar, Puthiya Tamilakam among Devendrar and Viduthalai Chiruthaigal Katchi among Paraiyar polled 12 percent vote in the 1999 Loksabha elections. After 1931, caste based census was not performed and hence the census data is not available for other castes.

CHRISTIANITY IN TAMIL NADU

Christianity in the state of Tamil Nadu, India is believed to be atleast 300 years and legendarily almost 2000 years old. Letters and several documents of Sixteenth century Jesuit Fathers indicate introduction of Christianity in Sixteenth century by St Francis Xavier in Kanyakumari District. According to tradition developed in 19th century, St. Thomas, one of the twelve apostles, landed in Malabar Coast (modern day Kerala) in AD 52. In the colonial age a large number of Portuguese, Dutch, British and Italian Christians came to Tamil Nadu. Priests accompanied them not only to minister the colonisers but also to spread the Christian faith among the non-Christians in Tamil Nadu. Currently, Christians are a minority community comprising 6% of the total population. Christians are mainly concentrated in the southern districts of Tamil Nadu - Kanyakumari (48.7% of the population, 2001), Thoothukudi (17%, 2001) and Tirunelveli (11%, 2001).

The Roman Catholic Church (Latin Rite), the Church of South India, the Syro-Malabar Catholic Church, the Syro-Malankara Catholic Church, the Malankara Orthodox Syrian Church, the Evangelical Church of India, the Pentacosts, the Apostolics, and other evangelical denominations constitute the Christian population in Tamil Nadu. The Latin Rite of Roman Catholic Church is the oldest and the largest among all. With

15 dioceses including the Roman Catholic Archdiocese of Madras and Mylapore and the Roman Catholic Archdiocese of Madurai, the Latin Rite has a homogeneous presence throughout the state.

San Thome Basilica, Chennai is built over the site where St.Thomas is believed to be originally interred

The second largest church by number of members is the Church of South India with 8 dioceses in Tamil Nadu. They are Coimbatore Diocese, Kanyakumari Diocese, Madras Diocese, Madurai-Ramnad Diocese, Thoothukudi - Nazareth Diocese, Tirunelveli Diocese, Trichy-Tanjore Diocese and the Vellore Diocese. Church of South India Synod, the highest administrative body of the Church of South India, is in Chennai. The vast majority of Christians in Tamil Nadu are either members of the Latin Rite Roman Catholic Church or the Church of South India. The Pentecostal Mission (TPM) is headquartered in Chennai.

In 1996, the Syro-Malabar Catholic Church created its first 'Diocese of Thuckalay' in Kanyakumari district, (which was under the Syro-Malabar Catholic Archdiocese of Changanassery in Kerala till then), of Tamil Nadu. The same year the Syro-Malankara Catholic Church has also newly established the 'Diocese of Marthandam' (bifurcated from its Archdiocese of Trivandrum) in Kanyakumari district. The Malankara Orthodox Syrian Church established its first diocese Chennai Diocese in the year 1979. St. Thomas Mount in Chennai, the place where St. Thomas, one of the disciples of Jesus Christ, was believed to have been martyred, is an important pilgrimage site for Indian Christians. The Santhome Basilica, supposedly built atop the tomb of St. Thomas, and the Vailankanni Basilica of Our Lady of Good Health—revered churches by India's Roman Catholics—are good examples of majestic church architectures in Tamil Nadu.

Kanyakumari Christians

Saint Thomas Christians some of whom are found in Kanyakumari are believed to be the oldest Christian community in the Indian Plains dating almost as per tradition 1900 years back. The religion was introduced according to tradition in 52 AD in the modern day Kanyakumari District by St. Thomas, the Apostle, one of the 12 Apostles of Jesus Christ who landed in Malabar Coast (modern day Kerala) in AD 52. They Traded with Greek, Jews and Persian Merchants in the Heyday of 11th century. Today, this ancient community is found though mainly in Kerala is also found in Tamil Nadu. Later the colonial age brought a large number of Portuguese, Dutch, British and Italian Christians to the district. Priests accompanied them not only to minister the colonisers but also to spread the Christian faith among the millions of non-Christians in Tamil Nadu.

Important Basilicas

Basilica of Our Lady of Good Health

The Basilica of Our Lady of Good Health is located in the small town of Velankanni in the state of Tamil Nadu in Southern India. The Roman Catholic Basilica is devoted to Our Lady of Good Health. Devotion to Our Lady of Good Health of Velankanni can be traced to the mid-16th century and is attributed to three miracles at different sites around where the Bacilica currently stands: the apparition of Mary and the Christ Child to a slumbering shepherd boy, the curing of a lame buttermilk vendor, and the rescue of Portuguese sailors from a violent sea storm.

Although all three apparitions ultimately resulted in the erection of a shrine to our Lady, it was the promise of the Portuguese sailors that was the proximate cause of a permanent edifice being built at Velankanni. The chapel was dedicated on the feast of the Nativity of the Blessed Virgin Mary (September 8), the day of their safe landing. More than 500 years later, the nine-day festival and celebration is still observed and draws nearly 5 million pilgrims each year. The Shrine of Our Lady of Vailankanni, also known as the "Lourdes of the East," is one of the most important Christian religious sites frequented by Christians in India.

San Thome Basilica

San Thome Basilica is a Roman Catholic (Latin Rite) minor basilica in Santhome, in the city of Chennai (Madras), India. It was built in the 16th century by Portuguese explorers, and rebuilt again with the status of a cathedral by the British in 1893. The British version still stands today. It was designed in Neo-Gothic style, favoured by British architects in the late 19th century. Christian tradition holds that St. Thomas arrived in Kerala in 52 A.D. preached between 52 A.D. and 72 A.D., when he was believed to be martyred on St. Thomas Mount. The basilica is built over the site where he was believed originally to be interred.

San Thome Basilica is the principal church of the Madras-Mylapore Catholic Archdiocese. In 1956, Pope Pius XII raised the church to the status of a Minor Basilica, and on February 11, 2006, it was declared a national shrine by the Catholic Bishops' Conference of India. The San Thome Basilica is a pilgrimage centre for Christians in India. The church also has an attached museum.

Poondi Madha Basilica

Our Lady of Lourdes Basilica, Poondi, is a Catholic pilgrimage centre located in Thanjavur, Tamil Nadu, South India. Poondi is a small village located in Thiruvaiyaru Taluk (also spelled as Taluka), about 35 km away from Thanjavur. It is considered as one of the Roman Catholic pilgrim centres similar to Velankanni, which houses the famous Poondi Madha Shrine that attracts pilgrims from all over India.

TAMIL MUSLIM

Tamil Muslims are Tamils who practise Islam. The community exists primarily in the Indian state of Tamil Nadu. Tamil-speaking Muslims in Sri Lanka are classified as Moors. The community is predominantly urban. There is a substantial diaspora, particularly in South East Asia, which has seen their presence as early as the 13th century. In the late 20th century, the diaspora expanded to North America and Western Europe.

Ethnic identity

Though numerically nominal, the community is not homogeneous. Its origin is shaped by miscegenation and centuries of trade between the Bay of Bengal and the Maritime Southeast Asia. By the 20th century, certain Tamil communities began to be listed as social classes in official gazettes of different nations as Marakayar, Rowther and Lebbai.

Economy

In Tamil Nadu, the community is well known as rentiers, entrepreneurs, gemstone jewellers and money changers with above State-average GDP per capita incomes.

Marakkayar

Claiming Arabic descent, the Marakayar sect has played a large role in the educational and economic landscape in Tamil Nadu since the 17th century. One notable sea-faring merchant, as recorded in the *Chronicles of Thondaiman*, was Periya Thambi Nainar Marakkayar who is widely believed to be the first rupee millionaire in the community. His son Seethakaathi, an altruist, commissioned the penning of Seerapuranam by Umaru Pulavar. By the 20th century, B. S. Abdur Rahman had emerged as the first dollar billionaire.

Culture

Legends and rituals

As a mark of modesty, women usually wear white *thuppatti* (whilst travelling only) which is draped over their body on top of the saree but revealing face. Many visit (Dargah) on major life milestones like births, marriages and deaths.

Keelakarai Jumma Masjid, built in 7th century, with prominent Tamil architectural characteristics, is one of the oldest mosques in Asia

Literature

The earliest Tamil Muslim literary works could be traced to the 14th century in the form of Palsanthmalai, a small work of eight stanzas. In 1572, Seyku Issaku, better known as Vanna Parimala Pulavar, published Aayira Masala Venru Vazhankum Adisaya Puranam detailing the Islamic principles and beliefs in a FAQ format. In 1592, Aali Pulavar wrote the Mikurasu Malai. The epic Seerapuranam by Umaru Pulavar is dated to the 17th century and still considered as the crowning achievement of Tamil Muslim literature. Other significant works of 17th century include Thiruneri Neetham by Sufi master Pir Mohammad, Kanakabhisheka Malai by Seyku Nainar Khan (alias Kanakavirayar), Tirumana Katchi by Sekathi Nainan and the Iraq war ballad Sackoon Pataippor.

Nevertheless, an independent identity evolved only in the last quarter of the 20th century triggered by the rise of Dravidian politics as well as the introduction of new mass communications and lithographic technologies. The world's first Tamil Islamic Literature Conference was held in Trichy in 1973. In early 2000. the Department of Tamil Islamic Literature was set up in the University of Madras. Modern notable writers include Mu Metha and Pavalar Inqulab,

Law and polity

Pre-independence

P. Kalifulla served as the minister for public works in the Cabinet of Kurma Venkata Reddy Naidu in 1937. He was sympathetic to the cause of Periyar E. V. Ramasamy and his Self-Respect Movement. He spoke against the introduction of compulsory Hindi classes in the Madras legislature and participated in the anti-Hindi agitations. He was a lawyer by profession and was known by the honorifics *Khan Bahadur*. He became the *Dewan* of Pudukottai after withdrawal from political work.

Sir Mohammad Usman was the most prominent among the early political leaders of the community. In 1930, Jamal

Mohammad became the president of the Madras Presidency Muslim League. Until then, the party was dominated by Urduspeakers. Yakub Hasan Sait served as a minister in the Rajaji administration. Allama Karim Gani, veteran freedom fighter and a close associate of Subash Chandra Bose, who hailed from Ilayangudi, served as Information Minister in Netaji ministry during the 1930s.

Post-independence

Since the late 20th century, politicians like Quaid-e-Millat (first President of Indian Union Muslim League) and Dawood Shahadvocated Tamil to be made an official language of India due to its antiquity in parliamentary debates

The community was united in a single political party under *Quaid-e-Millath* presidency for 27 years keeping rabble-rousers away until his death in 1972. Their support was invaluable for ruling parties in the state, as well as in the Centre. He was instrumental in framing and obtaining the minority status and privileges for minorities in India thus safeguarding the Constitution of India. His newspaper *Urimaikkural* was a very popular daily.

M. M. Ismail became Chief Justice in 1979 and was sworn in as Acting Governor of Tamil Nadu in 1980. As *Kamban Kazhagam* president, he organised literary festivals, that focussed on classical Tamil literature. Justice S. A. Kader who was the Judge of Madras High Court during 1983-89 became the President of Tamil Nadu State Government Consumer Disputes Redressal Commission on retirement.

In the early 1990s, the Indian National League split from the IUML. The non-denominational social reform movements (called Ghair Muqallid) began to take the front stage (supposedly to fight superstition creep) spearheaded by P. Jainulabdeen further weakening the IUML and causing unrest among community elders who preferred status quo and conservatism. Nevertheless, the Tamil Nadu Muslim Munnetra Kazagham was constituted in 1995. This non-profit organisation quickly became popular and assertive among the working class youth. Later, the Manithaneya Makkal Katchi, the political arm of TMMK was formed.

But TMMK itself split to form the break-away organisation Tamil Nadu Thowheed Jamath soon. MMK contested in three seats and won two Assembly seats *viz.* Ambur (A. Aslam Basha) and Ramanathapuram (M. H. Jawahirullah).

Broadly speaking, the community vote bank tends to support laissez faire and free trade; and have been unimpressed by Communism as a public policy though fringe working class factions often called for affirmative action in the last quarter of the 20th century.

21st century

New generation of leaders like Daud Sharifa Khanum have been active in pioneering social reforms like independent mosques for women.

MLAs and MPs such as A. Anwar Rhazza, J. M. Aaroon Rashid, Abdul Rahman, Jinna, Khaleelur Rahman, S. N. M. Ubayadullah, Hassan Ali and T. P. M. Mohideen Khan are found across all major Dravidian political parties like DMK, DMDK and AIADMK, as well as national parties like the INC.

At the age of 30, the award-winning documentarian Aloor Shanavas became the Deputy General Secretary of Viduthalai Chiruthaigal Katchi.

TAMIL JAIN

Tamil Jains are Tamils from Tamil Nadu, India, who practice Digambara Jainism (Tamil *CamaG□am*). They are a microcommunity of around 85,000 (around 0.13% of the population of Tamil Nadu). Tamil Jains are predominantly scattered in northern Tamil Nadu, largely in the districts of Madurai, Viluppuram, Kanchipuram, Vellore, Tiruvannamalai, Cuddalore and Thanjavur. Early Tamil-Brahmi inscriptions in Tamil Nadu date to the 3rd century BCE and describe the livelihoods of Tamil Jains.

Mel Sithamur Jain Math, the residence of Laxmisena

History

Origins

Some scholars believe that Jain philosophy must have entered South India some time in the sixth century BCE. Literary sources and inscription state that Bhadrabahu came over to Shravanabelagola with a 12,000-strong retinue of Jain sages when north India found it hard to negotiate with the 12-year long famine in the reign of Chandragupta Maurya. Even Chandragupta accompanied this constellation of sages. On reaching Shravanabelagola, Bhadrabahu felt his end approaching and decided stay back along with Chandragupta and he instructed the Jain saints to tour over the Chola- and Pandyan-ruled domains.

According to other scholars, Jainism must have existed in South India well before the visit of Bhadrabhu and Chandragupta.

A number of Tamil-Brahmi inscriptions have been found in Tamil Nadu that date from the second century BCE. They are regarded as associated with Jain monks and lay devotees.

The exact origins of Jainism in Tamil Nadu is unclear. However, Jains flourished in Tamil Nadu at least as early as the Sangam period. Tamil Jain tradition places their origins are much earlier. The Ramayana mentions that Rama paid homage to Jaina monks living in South India on his way to Sri Lanka. Some scholars believe that the author of the oldest extant work of literature in Tamil (3rd century BCE), Tolkâppiyam, was a Jain.

Tirukkural by Thiruvalluvar is considered by many to be the work of a Jain by scholars like V. Kalyanasundarnar, Vaiyapuri Pillai, Swaminatha Iyer, and P. S. Sundaram. It emphatically supports strict vegetarianism (or veganism) (Chapter 26) and states that giving up animal sacrifice is worth more than thousand burnt offerings (verse 259).

Silappatikaram, the earliest surviving epic in Tamil literature, was written by a SamaGa, Ilango Adigal. This epic is a major work in Tamil literature, describing the historical events of its time and also of then-prevailing religions, Jainism, Buddhism and Shaivism. The main characters of this work, Kannagi and Kovalan, who have a divine status among Tamils, were Jains.

According to George L. Hart, who holds the endowed Chair in Tamil Studies by University of California, Berkeley, has written that the legend of the Tamil Sangams or "literary assemblies", was based on the Jain *sangham* at Madurai:

There was a permanent Jaina assembly called a Sangha established about 604 A.D. in Madurai. It seems likely that this assembly was the model upon which tradition fabricated the Sangam legend.

Jainism became dominant in Tamil Nadu in the fifth and sixth century CE, during a period known as the *Kalabhra interregnum*.

Decline

Jainism began to decline around the 8th century A.D., with many Tamil kings embracing Hindu religions, especially Shaivism. Still, the Chalukya, Pallava and Pandyadynasties embraced

Jainism. The Shaivite legend about the impalement of the Jains in Madurai claims that 8000 Jains were impaled after they lost a contest against the Saivites, Thirugnana Sambandhar was invited by the queen of Madurai to check the atrocities of Jains and their influence on the King; however, this legend is not mentioned in any Jain text According to Paul Dundas, the story represents the abandonment of Madurai by Jains for economic reasons or the gradual loss of their political influence.

Archaeological evidences

The ruins of Anandamangalam vestiges were discovered in *Anandamangalam*, a small hamlet near *Orathi* village in Kancheepuram district of Tamil Nadu. The ruins had the rock-cut sculptures of *yakshini* (tutelary deity) Ambika and tirthankara Neminatha and Parshvanatha.

Population

The total number of Tamil Jains as per 2011 Indian census is 83,359, which forms 0.12% of the total population of Tamil Nadu (72,138,958).

Jains in Tamil Nadu

Parameter	Population	Male	Female
Total Population	83,359	43,114	40,245
Literates Population	68,587	36,752	31,835
Workers Population	26,943	23,839	3,104
Cultivators Population	2,216	1,675	541
Agricultural Workers Population	768	325	443
HH Industry Workers Population	574	441	133
Other Workers Population	23,385	21,398	1,987
Non-Workers Population	56,416	19,275	37,141

Lifestyle

The occupation of the majority of the Tamil Jain families is agriculture. Many are teachers. A considerable number of them are settled in urban areas, they are employed in public and private sectors. A small population has settled overseas (US, Canada, UK, Australia and other places).

Cuisine: Tamil Jains are ardent vegetarians. Until the turn of the 20th century, they were a self-sustained rural based farming community. They were landowners and used contract labourers for their agricultural activities. Their household included large tracts of land, cattle, and milch cows. They had kitchen gardens growing vegetables for their daily need. Dairy food such as milk, curd, butter and ghee were cooked in house. Daily food was very simple consisting of a brunch with rice, cooked lentils (paruppu), ghee, vegetable sambar, curd, sun dried pickles of mango, lemon or citron, deep fried sun dried 'crispies' (vadavam) made from rice pie. Evening snacks of deep fired lentil preparations and before sunset dinner consisting either idli, dosa or rice with buttermilk and lentil chutney (thogaiyal). While seniors, people undergoing religious fast and ardent followers of religious principles avoided garlic, onions and tubers in their daily food, these were occasionally used by others in the household.

Identity

Tamil Jains are well assimilated in Tamil society, without any outward differentiation. Their physical features are similar to Tamils. Apart from certain religious adherences, practices and vegetarianism, their culture is similar to the rest of Tamil Nadu. However, they name their children by the names of Tirthankaras and characters from Jaina literature.

Lifetime ceremonies

Ezhankaapu - on the seventh day of its birth, a new born baby is adorned with bracelets.

Kaathu Kutthal - ear piercing and adorning child with earrings. This ceremony is mostly performed in either Aarpakkam temple or Thirunarangkondai i.e.Thirunarungkundram. (Appandai Nathar is the deity).

Other Ceremonies

Upadesam - the formal induction into religious practices and adherences is called Upadesam. This is done to both boys and girls, at around the age of 15. After Upadesam, one is supposed to follow religious practices with vigor and seriousness.

Marriage - outwardly, Jain marriages resemble Hindu marriages. However, the mantras chanted are Jain. There is no Brahmin priest; instead there is a SamaGār called a *Koyil Vaadhiyar* or temple priest, who conducts the ceremonies.

Pilgrimage - most Jains go on pilgrimage to tirthas and major Jain temples in North India - Sammed Shikharji, Pavapuri, Champapuri and Urjayanta Giri - as well as places in South India such as Shravanabelagola, Humcha or Hombuja Humbaj, Simmanagadde in Karnataka and Ponnur Malai in Tamil Nadu.

There are private amateur tour operators as well who take pilgrims to newly identified ancient Tamil jain sites in western Tamil Nadu (kongunadu) and northern Kerala (vayanadu).

Funeral rites - the dead are placed on a pyre and incinerated. Ashes are then disbursed in water courses and ceremonies are performed on 10th or 16th day. Annual remembrance ceremonies similar to Hindu practice are not performed. But no festivities or functions are followed that year on the paternal side.

Festivals

- Akshaya Tritiya commemorates the first Tirthankara, Rishabha, partaking food after many long years of penance.
- Jinaratri commemorates Rishabha's moksha.
- Mahavir Jayanti celebrates Tirtankara Mahavira's birth.
- Diwali commemorates Mahavira's moksha.
- Vasant Panchami honors the Jain Agamas
- Upaakarma commemorates the Chakravartin Bharata, son of Rishabha, acknowledging the true scholars by awarding them the Upanayana.

- Karthikai Deepam at the onset of the month of Kartika
- Puthandu and Thai Pongal are the other common festivals celebrated along with other Tamils.

Fastings and other religious practices

Full moon days, Chaturdasi (14th day of the fortnight), Ashtami (8th day of the fortnight) are days chosen for fasting and religious observations. Women take food only after reciting the name of a tirthankara five times. People undertake such practices as a vow for certain period of time - sometimes even for years. On completion, Udhyapana festivals (special prayer services) are performed, religious books and memorabilia are distributed. People who take certain vows eat only after sunrise and before sunset.

9

Art, Architecture, Fair and Festivals

ARCHITECTURE OF TAMIL NADU

The Annamalaiyar Temple in Thiruvannaamalai

Tamil Nadu architecture that emerged thousands of years ago.

Rock-cut architecture

The Pallavas ruled from AD (600–900) and their greatest constructed accomplishments are the single rock temples in Mahabalipuram and their capital Kanchipuram, now located in Tamil Nadu.

Pallavas were pioneers of south Indian architecture. The greatest accomplishments of the Pallava architecture are the rock-cut temples at Mahabalipuram. There are excavated pillared halls and monolithic shrines known as rathas in Mahabalipuram. Mention must be made here of the Shore Temple constructed by Narasimhavarman II near Mahabalipuram which is a UNESCO World Heritage Site.

Chola architecture

The Chola kings ruled from AD (848–1280) and included Rajaraja Chola I and his son Rajendra Chola who built temples such as the Brihadeshvara Temple of Thanjavur and Brihadeshvara Temple of Gangaikonda Cholapuram, the Airavatesvara Temple of Darasuram and the Sarabeswara (Shiva)Temple, also called the Kampahareswarar Temple at Thirubhuvanam, the last two temples being located near Kumbakonam.

The first three among the above four temples are titled Great Living Chola Temples among the UNESCO World Heritage Sites.

The Cholas were prolific temple builders right from the times of the first king Vijayalaya Chola after whom the eclectic chain of Vijayalaya Chozhisvaram temple near Narttamalai exists.

Christian

San Thome Basilica is a Roman Catholic (Latin Rite) minor basilica in Santhome, in the city of Chennai (Madras), India. It was built in the 16th century by Portuguese explorers, and rebuilt again with the status of a cathedral by the British in 1893.

Temple Architecture

Tamil Nadu, the holy land, is the land of temple architecture. The Pallavas, Cholas, Pandyas, Vijayanagar rulers and the Nayakas have made immense contributions to temple art in Tamil Nadu.

Thousands of temples with lofty towers dot the skyline of the entire state of Tamil Nadu. The Tamils have been the greatest of temple builders. Temples from the pre Christian era as well as those from the 20th century exist in this state, where the ancient rulers have made outstanding contributions to the growth of these monuments of great artistic value.

Contributions Of The Pallava And Pandya Rulers

The cave temples of Pallavas and Pandyas were the beginning in temple architecture. This gave place to structural temples built with cut stones. These types of sculptural decoration are found at Mamandur, Tiruchirappalli and Pallavaram, which are attributed to Mahendravarman. The examples seen at Mamallapuram exhibit a striking variation from the cave temples with bas-reliefs, monoliths and cutout rocks, which were introduced by Mamalla Narasimhavarman I, son of Mahendravarman.

The Kailasanathar temple at Kanchipuram, the 'City Of Thousand Temples' and the shore temple at Mamallapuram are the best examples of structural temples, which replaced the rock medium. They are attributed to the eternal noble men Rajasimha and Narasimha Varman II during the same period.

Contributions Of The Chola Rulers

Followed by Pallavas, the Cholas continued their reign from the middle of the 9th century for over 500 years and established themselves as the superiors among all the dynasties in building mammoth places of worship. They brought significant changes in the structural style with multiple layers, towering 'Gopurams', 'Parivaras' and separate shrine for the goddess. During their period, the land was studded with temples. Their architectural achievement is the Brihadeeswarar temple at Thanjavur. The temples at Parasuram, Thiruverkadu, Kumbakonam, etc. are the best examples of the Cholas final phase, which was a fine degree of perfection in temple architecture.

Contributions Of The Vijayanagar Rulers

The Vijayanagar rulers made valuable additions to existing temples. They built many structures in a new style. The Gopurams became taller containing richness in sculptural details and the spacious 'Mandapams' became even larger. Their finest specimens are seen atSrirangam, Kanchipuram, Chidambaram and Tiruvannamalai.

Contributions Of The Nayak Rulers Of Madurai

The tallest temple towers at Srivilliputhur, Madurai, Rameswaram and Tirunelveli are the best in the tradition of the Nayak rulers of Madurai who continued the Vijayanagar example and improved the elegance.

TAMIL NADU ART AND CRAFTS

There is ample mention of the exquisite arts and crafts of Tamil Nadu in the chronicles of Pliny, Kautilya and other scholars who marvel at the states fine silk, soft muslin, ornate ivory work and precious stones like diamonds, rubies, pearls and tortoise shell. Tamil Nadu, resting at the pinnacle of ancient culture was the erstwhile kingdom of the Pallava, Pandya and Vijayanagar rulers and has ample relics that testify the architectural grandeur and the cultural efflorescence of the period.

Tamil Nadu, India's cultural capital is renown for its splendid temples and other architectural edifices. The state's claim to fame lies in its magnificent and renowned Tanjore paintings that thrived in ancient Tanjavoor during the Chola dynasty. The revered and traditional art form depicting the sacred deities is embellished with semi-precious stones, pearls, glass pieces and gold and colored in the vibrant hues. The modern Tanjore paintings however portray floral motifs, animals, birds as well as pretty human figures.

Tamil Nadu's art and culture also abounds in musical instruments that strike a melodious chord. The Naadaswaram, the Silappadikaaram, the Kumbu, Thambhuras and vcarious lutes and percussion instruments add a musical note to the various colorful festivities of the state.

VARIOUS ARTS & CRAFTS OF TAMIL NADU

Paintings

The Tanjore paintings are a hallmark of India's rich cultural legacy. Painted in vibrant shades embellished in colorful semi-precious stones, pearls, glass pieces and gold, they form some of the world's masterpieces done on surfaces of wood, mica or ivory. The paintings also adorn the ornate pillars, elaborately decorated canopies and garlands of ropes and chandeliers.

The unique style of Tangore paintings is an interesting subject of study. At its very inception, a wooden board is prepared. The paintings are done on a separate unbleached cloth and treated with a mixture of glue and chalk powder. Finally the drawing is traced on the board, followed by elaborate and exquisite embellishments and painted with an amalgam of chalk powder and gum arabica to produce three dimensional stylized shading effect that is truly a sight to behold.

Stone Carving

Tamil Nadu, the center of South India's cultural extravaganza had exhibited a distinctive brilliance in its stone carvings during the commencement days of ancient Indian history. This primordial craft achieved prominence because of the generosity of the culturally refined ancient sovereigns who patronized the talented local craftsmen and kept the art form alive.

Among the relics of Tamil Nadu's stone carvings that have been excavated from archeological sites, the granite figurines and statuettes deserve special mention. They narrate a sad tale of the vestiges of time. Contemporary granite carving is confined mainly around Mamallapuram and Chingleput, with the leading sculptors hailing from the local Vishwakarma or Kammaalar communities.

Woodcraft

Tamil Nadu, the epicenter of South India's cultural extravaganza is noted for a multitude of reasons ranging from its splendid temples, imposing monuments as well as an efflorescent art and culture manifested in its paintings, wood crafts and sculptures.

Woodcraft is a burgeoning revenue generating industry in Tamil Nadu. The state whose skilful craftsmen once depended upon the patronage of the ancient monarchs to earn their livelihoods is now teeming with talented local villages and artisans whose expertise is manifested in the variety of indigenous artifacts created by them.

Tamil Nadu's basket and fiber products are aesthetically appealing and very much in vogue all over the country and abroad. Palm trees along with bamboo shoots, cane, grass and reeds form a major ingredient of Tamil Nadu's wood works and relate basket products. Besides the wooden barks, the coconut fibers are used to make common utility products like baskets, ropes, mats and other miscellaneous items.

Jewellery

Tamil Nadu abounds in cultural splendor that is manifested in its efflorescent art and culture. The state has reached the zenith of cultural excellence and is noted for its traditional stone-encrusted jewelry that consists of earrings, nose drops, neckpieces, waist belts as well as anklets and bracelets.

No woman's trousseau is complete without a dash of sparkling jewelry. In ancient Tamil Nadu, diamonds and other precious stones were a man and woman's best friend alike. The people firmly believed in the magical wonders of the navaratnas or the nine gems that supposedly warded of the evil and magnified the favorable aspect of the planetary positions.

Making musical instruments

The art and culture of Tamil Nadu flourished under the benefaction of the ancient monarchs who were lovers of art and patronized the ancient craftsmen. Today it is a thriving revenue-generating industry and a source of livelihood of many.

Music and dance dominate Tamil Nadu's cultural scenario. A natural ramification of this led to the establishment of musical instrument making shops and industries. A vast majority of these centers are situated around Thanjavur, which has produced some of the country's leading musicians.

Pottery

India, a country where an underlying sense of unity abounds in diversity has a deep-rooted sense of tradition. Tamil Nadu, in southeast India occupies the pinnacle of the country's fine culture with its abundant traditional pottery, woodworks, paintings and jewelry.

South Indian culture, art and crafts flourished under the benefaction of the generous and intellectual rulers of the Pallava, Chola, Pandya and the Vijayanagar dynasties. Tamil Nadu, the country's cultural hot seat is renown for its magnificent temples and monuments that recount a tale of the country's historic grandeur and majestic splendor.

Archeologists have excavated relics of South Indian pottery. They are mainly made of terracotta moulds painted in a rich brown color. The ancient pottery reflects the country's legacy as well as the sophistication and cultural refinement of the ancient people.

FAIRS AND FESTIVALS IN TAMIL NADU

The state of Tamil Nadu is the origin of Dravidian culture. All the temples and monuments in the state are the best examples of Dravidian architecture. The state has made priceless contributions to the music, art, and literature of India. Bharatnatyam, one of the famous Indian dance forms, has its origin here. Tamil Nadu fairs and festivals are important events that happen round the year and lead to millions of footfalls from different corners of the world.

Tamil Nadu Fairs and Festivals: An Overview

All the fairs and carnivals in the state are observed with pomp and glory. Given below are some of the popular Tamil Nadu fairs and festivals:

Natyanjali Dance Festival

This festival takes place at Chidambaram, which is located beside the shoreline of the Bay of Bengal at a distance of 75 km from Pondicherry. The carnival begins from the day of Mahashivaratri and goes on for five days. The Natyanjali Dance Festival is the ideal means to pay tribute to Lord Nataraja, who is regarded as the lord of dancers. The Nataraj Temple is situated in a heavenly ambience.

Pongal

The Pongal is also known as the Harvest Festival. It is observed to offer homage to the Nature, Sun and Cattle for supporting people with a thriving harvest and affluence. The conventional cuisine of Pongal or boiled rice with milk and jaggery is made at every house.

Tourist Fair Chennai

This fair in Chennai makes you familiar with the cultural resources, tourist attractions, and economic situation of Tamil Nadu. It is usually held in January.

Chithirai Festival Madurai

The renowned Madurai temple is the home to this event, which is approximately 500 km from Chennai.

This colorful event begins from the start of the Tamil month of Chithirai and concludes on the 10th day of the month. The event is a magnificent rebuilding of the wedding of Princess Meenakshi of the Pandyas to Lord Sundareswarar.

Dance Festival Mamallapuram

This event starts on December 25th of each year and is celebrated on all Saturdays. Outdoor stages have been constructed approximately 1,300 years back. The remarkable monolithic stony carvings of the Pallava rulers are located beside the sea in the prehistoric city of Mamallapuram. This occasion is a true visual feast for the dance lovers. Dances performed include Bharatha Natyam, Kathakali, Kuchipudi, and Odissi.

Mahamagam

This event is a sacred occasion that draws one to Kumbakonam once in every 12 years. Kumbakonam is known as the city of temples.

Aurbathimoovar

The expression "Arubathimoovar" factually denotes the 63 saints of Shiva, worshipped for living admirable lives of dedication and atonement. Bronze statues of the 63 saints adorn the spectacular Kapaliswar temple at Mylapore, Chennai. Once every year, these statues are taken out in a vibrant parade through the roads of Mylapore.

Summer Festivals

These carnivals take place in the various picturesque hill stations of the state. During this time, the hills get a new look. Adventure sports, cultural events, flower shows, and boat races increase the vigor of the event.

Saral Vizha (Kuttalm or Courtallm)

The Sarai Vizha is just a customary way of bathing. Definitely, a bath at the beautiful Courtallam waterfalls is no everyday affair. The healing waters of the boisterous fall are renowned for their therapeutic characteristics.

Kanthuri Festival

The state of Tamil Nadu is a truly cosmopolitan state with

different cultures, religion, races and customs. This exceptional character has given birth to many colorful festivals and carnivals.

Among these, the Kanthuri Festival of Tamil Nadu is a symbol of secularism in the state as well as in the country. The unique feature of the Kanthuri Festival is that it is enjoyed and observed by the Hindus, Muslims and people of all other faiths alike.

Held at the shrine of Saint Quadirwali, the Kanthuri Festival act as the platform to choose the spiritual leader of the celebrations from one of the descendants of the saint. Amid elaborate rituals and rites, the devotees present their offerings to the Peer. The tenth and the last day of the festival witnesses the anointment of the tomb of the saint Quadirwali with sandalwood paste. Then the paste is distributed among the followers. It is believed that the paste has magical healing power.

Kavadi Festival

One of the most exciting festivals in India, the Kavadi Festival of Tamil Nadu is a blend of faith, sacrifice, glamor and custom. The extreme pain and sacrifice, a devotee undergoes to offer his prayers to Lord Muruga is known as the Kavadi. It is believed, the amount of virtue one receives by performing the Kavadi is million time greater than the pain he suffers. A Kavadi is a generally a wooden stick, which has two baskets hanging from it. The Kavadi that is carried by the bearers in their shoulders may vary in shapes and sizes. The Kavadis are adorned with peacock feathers and numerous brass bells. The two baskets are usually filled with rice, milk or any other things, which the devotee has promised to offer the Lord in his Vow.

The Kavadi bearer has to observe different rules from the time he has picked up the Kavadi till the day of the offering. One of the most difficult Kavadi offerings is the Agni Kavadi, where the devotee has to walk over a pit of burning coals while carrying the Kavadi. Egged by the watching crowd and boosted by the beating drums and fragrance of the burning incense sticks, the Kavadi bearer ecstatically walks through the red hot coals.

Velankanni

The Velankanni Festival of Tamil Nadu is surrounded by many mysterious legends. The most popular story is that some shipwrecked Portuguese sailors were saved miraculously from a terrible storm in the sea. After they had reached the shore, the local fishermen took them to a dilapidated chapel to thanks the god for saving their live. The sailors paid their tribute by establishing a permanent church. They worked on the improvement of the church with their subsequent visits.

Navrathri

Navrathri is celebrated in this state in a slightly different manner. Dolls, also known as Golu, are made and put on display.

Karthigai Deepam

It is also named as the "Festival of Lights" and it is one of the most colorful carnivals in the state. Karthigai Deepam is a very old event in Southern India which takes place on a full moon day. Small lamps are lit by people, embodying the Agni Linga.

Thyagaraja Music Festival

This Carnatic music carnival is held at Thiruvariyar. It takes place every year. The fiesta started to pay tribute to Saint Thyagaraja and is a treat for music lovers.

10

Education

EDUCATION PROFILE

Tamil Nadu has a history that dates back to a thousand years or more. Tamil Nadu prides from the fact that the first engineering institution to come into being in the country was the Survey School established in 1794 at Chennai by the East India Company.

Out of this grew the reputed College of Engineering, Guindy, and Chennai. Having made great strides in the field of Technical Education, Tamil Nadu is a frontline state in India imparting education in the field of technology.

The State Government has undertaken several programmes to overcome the problem of rural illiteracy and providing free elementary education among the masses. Schools in Tamil Nadu are either affiliated with the State Board or the Central Board of Secondary Education (CBSE).

Tamil is the medium of instruction and study in the rural schools of Tamil Nadu. The State has a literacy rate of 74% which is satisfactory as compared to the average literacy rate of the country.

Major cities like Chennai, Coimbatore, Trichi and Madurai are famous for their renowned educational institutions and research centres.

LIST OF UNIVERSITIES

1. Alagappa University, Tamil Nadu
2. Amrita Vishwa Vidyapeetham, Tamil Nadu
3. Annamalai University, Tamil Nadu
4. Avinashlingam Institute for Home Science & Higher Education for Women, Tamil Nadu
5. Bharathidasan University, Tamil Nadu
6. Bharthiar University, Tamil Nadu
7. Gandhigram Rural Institute, Tamil Nadu
8. Karunya Institute of Technology and Sciences, Tamil Nadu
9. Madurai Kamaraj University, Tamil Nadu
10. Manonmaniam Sundaranar University, Tamil Nadu
11. Mother Teresa Women's University, Tamil Nadu
12. National Institute of Technology, Tamil Nadu
13. Periyar University, Tamil Nadu
14. Shanmugha Arts, Science, Technology & Research Academy, Tamil Nadu
15. Sri Chandrasekharendra Saraswathi Viswa Mahavidyalaya, Tamil Nadu
16. Tamil Nadu Agricultural University, Tamil Nadu
17. Tamil University, Tamil Nadu
18. Thiruvalluvar University, Tamil Nadu
19. Vellor Institute of Technology, Tamil Nadu
20. Vinayaka Mission's Research Foundation, Tamil Nadu

TAMIL NADU BOARD OF SECONDARY EDUCATION

Tamil Nadu Board of Secondary Education, established in 1910, is under the purview of the Department of Education, Government of Tamil Nadu, India. Up to and ending at the secondary (class 10) level, the following streams of education are offered: the SSLC (Secondary School Leaving Certificate) stream, the Anglo-Indian stream, the Oriental School Leaving Certificate (OSLC) stream and the Matriculation stream.

And for higher secondary (classes 11 and 12) there is single unified stream leading to the award of the Higher Secondary Certificate (HSC). The Tamil Nadu State Board of School Examination evaluates students' progress by conducting two board examinations-one at the end of class 10 and the other at the end of class 12. The scores from the class 12 board examinations are used by universities to determine eligibility and as a cut-off for admissions into their programmes.

The jurisdiction of the board extends to schools located in the state of Tamil Nadu. Schools can choose to affiliate themselves to the Tamil Nadu Board of Secondary Education or to other boards-the CBSE or the ICSE-that are authorized to conduct secondary (class 10) and higher secondary (class 12) final examinations and award certificates to successful candidates.

Bibliography

Basham, A.L.: *A Cultural History of India*, Oxford, Clarendon Press, 1975.

Chaudhary, M.: *Partition and the Curse of Rehabilitation*, Calcutta, Bengal Rehabilitation Organization, 1964.

Chopra, P.N.; Ravindran, T.K.; Subrahmanian, N: *History of South India (Ancient, Medieval and Modern)* New Delhi: Chand Publications. 1934.

Delmonico, Neal: *Religions of India in Practice*, Princeton, Princeton University Press, 1995.

Desai, Mahadev : *Gandhi and Indian Villages*, New Delhi, Mohit Pub., 2002.

Duboi, Abbe: *Hindu Manners, Customs and Ceremonies*, Fifth Indian Impression, CUP, 1985.

Frauwallner, E..: *History of Indian Philosophy*, Motilal, Delhi, 1973.

Gambhirananda, S.: *Brahma Sutra Shamkar Bhasya,* Adavita Ashrama, Calcutta, 1977.

Gupta, N., and Satish Gupta: *Sarojini Naidu's Select Poems, with an Introduction, Notes, and Bibliography for Further Study.*Bareilly: Prakash Book Depot, 1976.

Hardy, Adam: *Indian Temple Architecture: Form and Transformation-The Karnata Dravida Tradition 7th to 13th Centuries*. Abhinav Publications. 1995.

Harle, J.C : *The art and architecture of the Indian Subcontinent*. New Haven, Conn: Yale University Press. 1994.

Hazra, Kanai Lal: *The Rise and Decline of Buddhism in India.* Munshiram Manoharlal: South Asia Books, 1995.

Hussein, Abdullah : *Downfall by Degrees,* New Delhi, Katha, 2004.

Ira Mervin Lapidus, *Muslim Cities in the Later Middle Ages,* Cambridge, Mass, 1967.

Jacob, K.: *Religion and Ethics in Advaita*, C.M.S. Press, Kottayam, 1982.

Jain, K. C.: *Bharatiya Digambar Jain Abhilekh.* Madhya Pradesh: Digambar Jain Sahitya Samrakshan Samiti, 2001.

Kalika Prasad Tiwari: *Foundations of Ancient Indian Culture*, Pointer Publishers, Delhi, 2001.

Kalindi Randeri: *Narendra Modi : The Architect of A Modern State*, Rupa, Delhi, 2009.

Keay, John. *India: A History*. New York: Grove Publications, 2000.

Krishna Murari: *The Calukyas of Kalyani, from circa 973 A.D. to 1200 A.D.*, Delhi, Concept, 1977.

Krishna Rao M. V.; *Studies in Kautilya*, Munshiram Manoharlal, Delhi, 1979.

Levinson, D.: *Family Violence in Cross Cultural Perspective*, Newbury Park, Sage, 1989.

Masica, Colin P. *The Indo-Aryan Languages.* Cambridge: Cambridge University Press, 1991.

Mayer, A.: *Caste in an Indian Village: Change and Continuity 1954-1992*, Delhi, OUP, 1996.

Metcalf, Thomas R.: *Modern India: An Interpretive Anthology*, London, Macmillan, 1971.

Misra, Satya Swarup: *The Aryan Problem: A Linguistic Approach*, Munshiram Manoharlal, New Delhi, 1992.

Mookerjee R. R.: *Local Government in Ancient India*, Oxford University Press, 1920.

Narasimhacharya, R. *History of Kannada Literature.* New Delhi, Madras: Asian Educational Services, 1988.

Parel , J.: *Hind Swaraj or Indian Home Rule*, Cambridge University Press, 1925.

Rao, B. S. L. Hanumantha : *The Age of Satavahanas.* Andhra Pradesh Sahitya Akademi, 1976.

Sastri, Nilakanta K. A. *A history of South India from prehistoric times to the fall of Vijayanagar.* New Delhi: Indian Branch, Oxford University Press, [1955] (2002).

Swami Vishnu Tirtha: *Devatma Shakti*, Swami Shivom Tirth, Rishikesh, 1962.

Index

S

T

V

W

❑❑❑

www.ingramcontent.com/pod-product-compliance
Ingram Content Group UK Ltd.
Pitfield, Milton Keynes, MK11 3LW, UK
UKHW042016290726
14061UKWH00001BB/22